With sincere good wishes

David Crawford

STANLEY
WOODS

THE WORLD'S FIRST MOTORCYCLE SUPERSTAR

by

David Crawford

First published 2012

ISBN 978-0-957034-10-5

Published by
David Crawford

Printed by Nicholson & Bass Ltd

CONTENTS

Dedicated to the memory of my friend
double side-car TT Winner

LOWERY BURTON
(1937–2010)

Edited by DAVID WRIGHT

THANKS TO THE FOLLOWING:

Sponsors
Raymond Crawford, Eamon Crawford, John Kidd,
Tony Steele, Thirty Motorcycle Club of Ulster &
Vintage Motor Cycle Northern Ireland Sections.

Acknowledgements
PAUL ADAMS
MARCO BJERKEN
DERMOT BYRNE
ROB COLENBRANDER
MARIO COLOMBO
PAUL D'ORLÉANS
BO EKLUND
AUGUSTO FARNETI
SIMON GREGSON
MOTOBILD ESSO & IRENE GUNNERSON
JOHN HARRISON
IVAR & AMY HERL
JOHN KIDD
MALMO SPORTS MUSEUM
NEVILLE McCONNOLL
DAVE McMAHON
NATIONAL MUSEUMS NORTHERN IRELAND
DENIS QUINLAN
ELWIN ROBERTS
BILL SNELLING (FOTO FINDERS)
HEATHER STAFFORD

Proof and Typing
LORRAINE CHEADLE
EAMON CRAWFORD
JOAN CRAWFORD

INTRODUCTION

HERE IS A BOOK which someone had to write, as a richly deserved tribute to one who made a remarkable contribution to motorcycle sport between the wars.

In the days when the word superstar was virtually unknown, here was a sportsman who could justify that description, especially for his performances in the Isle of Man. Between 1922 and 1939 he entered in thirty-seven TTs, won ten, retired whilst leading three more and was beaten in three more by a total of 48 seconds. He retired sixteen times, never finished lower than sixth and made eleven fastest laps. He also had an impressive continental Grand Prix record.

For many years, it was my great pleasure and privilege to know Stanley and his wife Mildred, enjoying their kindness and hospitality, as well as trips to England, the Isle of Man and Italy for special events. To add to this enjoyment were his kindly disposition, encyclopedic knowledge and a personality rarely to be met with and certainly never to be forgotten by the writer.

During his career Stanley rode British and foreign machines, won seven Ulster Grand Prix, and was very successful in many important events as an off-road rider (as late as 1968). He was the first motorcyclist to be invited to join the Texaco Hall of Fame. Wherever and whatever he rode, he was always outstanding, perhaps the greatest rider of his era, enjoying a glittering racing career that ended in 1939 with the outbreak of the Second World War.

He was a founder member and Past President of the TT Riders' Association and rode in Parade Laps up until he was eighty years old. No rider in the inter-war period rode in more TTs than Stanley Woods; he had great powers of recollection and a store of information which his advancing years had not dimmed in the least until his death in 1993, his ninetieth year. This book has provided the opportunity to tell the story of a remarkable man and to present a large number of associated photographs and illustrations to maximum advantage, many of historic significance including excerpts from private recordings, correspondence and personal records.

David Crawford
2012

Artist, cartoonist and journalist, Jock Leyden

FROM The Daily News
To-day's News To-day
P.O. BOX 1491, DURBAN

PER LUGPOS
BY AIR MAIL
PAR AVION

STANLEY WOODS, ESQ.,
17 BRIGHTON VALE,
MONKSTOWN,
DUBLIN,
EIRE.

My favourite machine! On this machine I put the cat among the pigeons in 1935! Stanley Woods

FOREWORD

I CONSIDER IT a great honour to be asked to write this Foreword on one of my great heroes – Stanley Woods.

I had the privilege of his support at the TTs and also before that I competed against him in grass tracks. After he retired from road racing in 1939 he was still a great competitor and enjoyed his trials and grass tracking immensely. In grass tracks he was always the man to beat with his stylish feet up riding.

Stanley rode in most of the Championship Trials in Ireland and he also loved the fearsome Scott Trial in Yorkshire. Unfortunately on his last effort at the Scott Trials he broke a leg which was the only breakage he had in his long racing career.

Sammy with the Museum's 1920 Brough

Stanley was a great tactician and also a great meticulous rider and was probably the first man to set up his own signals around the TT course so that he could know what the opposition were up to, and, needless to say this won him many TTs because of the advantage he had over his competitors.

Stanley rode a great array of bikes and was highly respected throughout the motorcycle factories of Europe. Moto Guzzi, DKW, Husqvarna, Norton, Velocette, BSA, James and Cotton to name but a few were some of the famous manufacturers which he rode for and won.

Stanley was a great personality and often made a late grand appearance at functions and dinners! I remember one such dinner where the great George Meier was the top guest and Stanley kept him waiting for an hour before he eventually turned up!

In later years Stanley had his Moto Guzzi business in Dublin which Moto Guzzi were very proud of, he also was very much into his wine making and had many a great confrontation with Rex McCandess at who was the best wine maker!

We still have some great memorabilia from Stanley in our Museum Trust, of which we are deeply honoured. He truly was one of the greats and a legend that lives on.

Sammy Millar
2012

STANLEY WOODS was born on 28th November 1903 at 21 Brighton Avenue Rathmines, a quiet residential area on the south side of Dublin. His parents Edward Hall Woods (Ted) and Elizabeth Menzies nee Stanley (Lily), a middle income family with a two year old daughter, Violet, were members of the Unitarian Church.

1904 Edward Hall Woods with baby Stanley

With older sister Violet

Since 1902 Ted was a commercial traveller and represented some very good English companies, Mackintosh Toffee of Halifax and Bassett Liquorice Allsorts of Sheffield. He then covered the whole thirty-two counties; this was before the partition of Ireland into two separate territories in 1922. (Six counties of Ulster which remained as part of the United Kingdom and twenty-six counties of the new Irish Free State).

His mother Lily owned an employment agency up until the 1950s in South Ann St. and later, in Dawson St., opposite the Mansion House, Dublin.

At about three of four years of age Stanley remembered moving to a bigger three storey house in Rathgar Square. Barely recalling kindergarten, his first experience of school was Norfolk College, Rathgar, which was really a girls' school.

When he was eight years old the Woods family advanced still further to what might be called the 'suburbs,' going to live in a very nice semi-detached house standing in its own grounds in Howth, about nine miles out of the city on the north shore of Dublin Bay.

At this time Stanley was enrolled in Mountjoy School, which was quite close to a railway station which the family used. One of the organisations he was in was the Boy Scouts who did not have a meeting room. They met in a small wood and had permission, if the weather was really bad, to take cover under the veranda of the local tennis club's pavilion.

Sutton 1916

1919 Cadet days

Despite belonging to the Boy Scouts, at this period in his life, he never felt part of a team and tended to be a loner, taking no part in organised sport.

Stanley was beginning to rebel against religion and after about a year at Mountjoy School his father knew he was very unhappy. Although it was not by any means a religious institution, the headmaster was a Reverend gentleman.

As far as Stanley was concerned, they seemed to concentrate too much on religious instruction. His father took him away from Mountjoy and sent him to another school situated on the South side of the city.

In 1916, when Stanley was thirteen, the family moved again, this time to Sutton, also on Dublin's North Shore. Here he was fortunate to make friends with another lad who was three years older. This friend had a 5/6hp Indian motorcycle and taught Stanley to ride, although a big difficulty was that there was little petrol available, it

being during the First World War. Another friend was serving an apprenticeship in the Great Southern Railway workshops in Dublin and somehow or another, through him, a two gallon tin of petrol arrived every month. However, after about another year the family moved back to Dublin and it was another three years before he had any more involvement with motorcycles.

Stanley had in the meantime joined the Cadets, which in those days before Irish independence meant the British Army Cadets.

As well as receiving normal training and parading, one day they were taken to an airfield, boarded for a flight in a Bomber and each given a leather helmet. Stanley managed to keep his and used it during his early days as a motorcyclist and for some of his first competitions, including his debut road race, the Banbridge 50.

He recalled a less enjoyable experience which occurred when he was about sixteen years old. He came across a crowd gathered in Sackville Street (later O'Connell Street) to listen to political speeches. In what were troubled times in Ireland, Stanley, wearing his Cadet uniform, was walking on the other side of the street and was chased by the crowd. Managing to evade them, he felt lucky to have escaped with his life. Despite his narrow escape, the following week he went to the same location to a mass meeting addressed by the Countess Markiewicz and was impressed by this charismatic speaker.

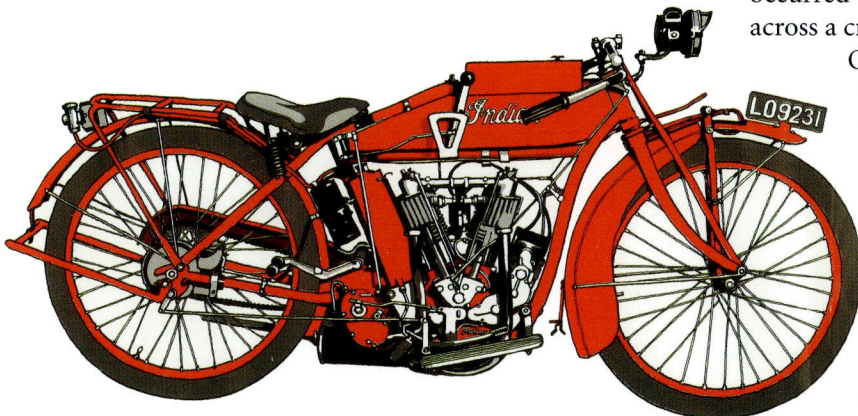

Indian 5/6 HP

1919 with Sun Vitesse

First motorcycle Sun Vitesse

For a sixteen year old the open road was beckoning and in the summer of 1919, he persuaded his mother Lily to buy him a motorcycle, a little single speed 2 ½hp Sun Vitesse, capable of perhaps 35 m.p.h. It was second-hand but looked absolutely brand new and cost £45. The name Vitesse springs from the initials of the actual engine manufacturers – The V.T.S. (Valveless Two Stroke) Company of Birmingham – which had been associated with Sun since 1913. Stanley would also have an association with this company up to the 1950s.

He rode this little machine to the limit and in 1920 entered his first ever motorcycle event – The Dublin and District Motorcycle Club's St. Patrick's Day Trial, starting at Donnybrook Bridge on the south side of the City, with a route leading via Cornell's Court to the luncheon stop at Glendalough, Co Wicklow. The hill from Cornell's Court to Carrickmines proved too much for the Sun and having partaken of a heavy breakfast, to fortify him for the anticipated rigours of the day, Stanley was unable to run alongside in accordance with the practices of the day. Completely puzzled by the lack of power, he decided to follow an easier route and was inspired to call upon an acquaintance. Within reasonable time, a case of slipped timing was diagnosed and was very quickly rectified. When he finally reached Glendalough, the last competitor had been despatched towards Dublin, so he set off towards home, later reading the results of the Trial in the newspaper.

He graduated from the Sun to a belt driven, hub-geared 3½ hp Triumph, of doubtful age but which was reputed to have seen service in France during the 1914-18 war. During this time he was attending Dublin High School, Rathgar, but not progressing very well with his studies, so at Easter 1920 he persuaded his father that he should leave school and follow him into the same business as a traveller.

A few weeks earlier during one of his trips around Dublin, he had seen the most fabulous Harley Davidson and sidecar in the window of the main agents Wayte Brothers of Lemon Street, just off Grafton Street. Ted was persuaded by his son to purchase the outfit, on the basis that Stanley would drive him the length and breadth of Ireland, selling his wares. On taking delivery of the Harley, the salesman realised that Stanley had little or no experience of driving such a powerful machine and sidecar, so suggested that he should have some instruction from their senior apprentice C. W. Johnston later known in motorcycling circles as Paddy. This was a fortunate move, for Stanley and Paddy became firm friends and it led to his introduction to motorcycle competition.

Hub-geared 3¹/2 hp Triumph

IN THE SPRING of 1921 political conditions in Ireland were very unsettled and the Irish War of Independence was ongoing. As Woods senior worked as a manufacturer's representative at the time, it was essential for him to have a reliable means of transport for his business and it was Stanley's job to chauffeur his father from customer to customer in the Harley outfit.

During those troubled times, the authorities imposed restrictions on travel, which limited people to journeys of no more than about twenty miles from home. In spite of all these difficulties trade went on nevertheless.

As the Harley was being used less for business because of the travel restrictions, it became more available for competition. Stanley managed to talk his father into allowing him to enter the machine for the Glen Cullen Hill climb, which was organised by The Dublin and District Motorcycle Club in May. With little regard for the fact that the Harley had to be available for work on Monday, Stanley showed his competitive spirit by taking third place overall and setting the fastest time of the day in the sidecar class.

At that time Stanley knew very little about the Isle of Man TT races until one day, when he was visiting the Rudge Retail Depot in St Stephen's Green, Dublin, he saw a little book which gave an account of Cyril Pullin's win in the 1914 Senior TT on a Rudge. The book referred to the race as the *Blue Riband of Motorcycle Sport.* Stanley did not know much about the TT and had

Stanley and Jack Duggan

never heard the phrase *Blue Riband* before, but he made some enquiries and discovered that a group of motorcycle enthusiasts were travelling from Dublin to the TT races the very next week. Stanley and Paddy Johnston joined them and took the Harley 'solo.' They sailed from Dun Laoghaire (Kingstown in those days) to Holyhead and then took the train to Liverpool where they got the boat to the Isle of Man. The evening before the race they went around the course to look for a good spot to watch the racing from.

The gates had to be opened and closed (by the pillion passenger) at East Mountain and at Keppel Gate but they decided to watch the race at Hillberry, a fast right-hander at the bottom of the Mountain descent. About halfway through the following day's race Stanley turned to Paddy and said "I could do that." Paddy said more or less the same thing.

Keppel Gate

Hillberry

Remembering Stanley's early association with the spot, in the late 1980s the TT Marshalls Association unveiled a hardwood seat at Hillberry in his memory. The 1921 Senior TT was won by Howard Davies (of HRD fame) riding an AJS 350cc. This is the only occasion that a rider has won the "Senior" on a "Junior" machine. Davies headed off the foreign challenge of Freddie Dixon and Bert le Vack who were both mounted on Indians, with a winning time of 4 hours 9 minutes and 22 seconds, a margin of only 2 minutes and 3 seconds over Dixon in the six-lap race.

Howard Davies 1921 Senior TT Winner

Only those who have travelled to the Isle of Man to watch a TT could imagine how the young Stanley might have felt. No thoughts of competing had crossed his mind until that day, Thursday 16th June, whilst sitting on a wall at Hillberry. That Senior event of 1921 was one of the most exciting TT races ever run and it inspired Stanley. He returned to Douglas that evening absolutely determined that the following year's start list would have his name on it. Stanley's pal Paddy was similarly inspired and he also went on to TT success himself.

Despite his new found interest in road racing, it was at the 1921 August Bank Holiday trial organised by the Dublin & District Motorcycle Club that Stanley won his first Gold Medal of many. Stanley went on to compete with great success in off-road trials events for many years but it is for his prowess in road racing that he is most famous.

His friend Paddy Johnston had, by then, completed his apprenticeship and along with a business partner had opened a motorcycle showroom. One of the firms for which they acted as agents was the Cotton Motorcycle Company. Stanley occasionally got a ride on one of their little side-valve machines. It so happened that there was an event coming up in mid-September in Northern Ireland, a speed trial at Magilligan Strand in Co. Derry. Paddy and his partner were entered, so Stanley and a party of supporters travelled the one hundred and seventy odd miles north to watch his friend compete. It turned out that Paddy's partner was overly fond of alcohol and when he broke down during the race, he promptly made for the nearest pub. Stanley made repairs to the machine, a New Scale, and along with Paddy on a Cotton, set off to ride back to Dublin.

They stopped at Banbridge in County Down to effect some repairs and whilst they were stopped, they were approached by some young motorcycle enthusiasts. The lads had spotted the race exhausts on the bikes, so they asked Paddy and Stanley if they would like to compete in a race they were helping to organise in a fortnight's time. Stanley asked them to send entry forms and these duly arrived a few days later.

As Paddy was in the trade he was assured of the use of a machine to compete on, but they needed a ruse to secure a machine for Stanley. Paddy came round to the Woods home to ask if he could use Stanley's father's fountain pen. Woods senior asked what he needed the

pen for and Paddy explained that he wanted to fill in his entry form for a race in Northern Ireland. Woods senior asked his son if he was not riding. Stanley said he had no machine and his father asked him what was wrong with the Harley. *"Nothing!"* was the reply and that is how Stanley Woods came to compete in his first road race, the Banbridge 50 on 29th September 1921.

At weekends, when his father did not need the use of the outfit, Stanley would detach the sidecar and use the Harley as a solo machine. He would also cold bend the handlebar into a sportier position for solo riding and bend them back after the event and re-attach the sidecar. Cold bending too often will lead to metal fatigue and during the Banbridge race the inevitable happened. Now nearly eighteen years old, with thick curly hair, thin but strong shoulders and a great physique, he had undertaken a course of physical training with an ex-army PT instructor whom he had met during his time as a Cadet. One day the instructor noticed Stanley smoking and threatened that if he did not give up smoking immediately, he would have nothing more to do with him. He justified the demand by explaining his reasons and as they sounded sensible to Stanley, he never smoked again.

STANLEY'S WORDS
BANBRIDGE 50 - 29th September

"I rode in the first Banbridge 50, my first road race on a 1000cc Harley Davidson, I was seventeen and with no experience. The Handicappers hit me hard; I got one minute from scratch, Jimmy Shaw on a Norton with Herbie Chambers on a works 350 AJS, thirty seconds behind me. I was not passed until my handlebar broke half way round the third lap (five laps of ten miles), that put me out of the race but lit the flame of enthusiasm that still burns."

A bystander cut a one inch thick branch out of a holly tree and tied it across the handlebar as a splint. Stanley completed his third lap, only to find by that time the race was over. The repair held until he got home to Dublin, that evening.

In local events during those early days, Jimmy Shaw was the idol of the crowds and was also the Ulster Distributor for Norton. Herbie Chambers was another great competitor, whose father William J Chambers ran a very successful motorcycle business. He was the AJS and BSA representative in Belfast and also a great supporter of the sport. Sadly Herbie Chambers lost his life whilst competing at Portmarnock Strand, Co. Dublin in 1925. Portmarnock Strand was very popular and the Flying Mile, the 5 Mile and the 25 Mile Irish Championship events were major fixtures on the

Father and son relaxing

Painting by Matthew Rodgers courtesy of National Museums Northern Ireland

calendar. Unfortunately, that fatal accident eventually put paid to strand racing at Portmarnock.

The following months were a time of worry to the budding racer, for Stanley realised that getting a suitable machine for road racing was not going to be an easy matter. He had virtually no experience in racing and was wary of what his parents might think of his new found ambitions. However, he was confident that he was no worse off than any other young TT hopeful, and set about finding a solution.

The classic way for a Motorcycle Manufacturer to sell their machines was through racing success. All the factories listed racing machines in their line-ups. These were typically overhead valve sports models with standard frames, sidecar lugs and would be road legal – complete with number plates as competitors nearly

With Violet

always rode to and from events. Race success virtually guaranteed increased sales and winning at the TT was every factory's biggest aim, for its success would receive worldwide publicity. It was a time when it was bad business not to race and good business to win.

Despite the problems involved, Stanley was determined to ride in the 1922 TT and after sounding out various sources and some deep thought he came up with a plan. He confided in Paddy Johnston that he was going to write to the manufacturers to offer his services. Paddy told him he was wasting his time as he had tried the same approach. He had received replies from them all but these just gave the details of the local agents where the various race machines could be bought. That was of no help to Stanley, for he had no money, but his plan was to write to manufacturers of certain "Senior" machines and tell them that he was entered in the Junior race and that he would also like to ride in the Senior race. Similar letters were sent to companies specialising in the manufacture of "Junior" machines. These letters claimed that the Indian agent in Dublin had entered him in the Senior TT and as a result he got replies from everyone. They all wanted to know who he was and what he had done. Stanley cleverly wrote back to them to the effect that "Self praise is no praise" and if they wanted to know more about him they should write to the president of the Dublin & District Motorcycle Club and to the local Indian agent.

Years later he disclosed that he was the person who actually dictated the replies to these letters.

1922

The reply from the Cotton Motorcycle Company seemed interesting and to hold out the most hope, so Stanley decided to concentrate on them.

He told them very little in an attempt to create an impression of modesty rather than his lack of experience. Negotiations dragged on until Easter 1922, with one of the most pressing problems being that of finance. Stanley proposed to Cotton that he would pay his entry fee and his own expenses if they would lend him a machine for the Junior race. Stanley reckoned that he would have to raise about fifty pounds. The entry fee would cost him twenty guineas and insurance would be another ten. The remainder of his costs would be mainly for travel to the island and his hotel accommodation during the races.

He would raise some of the £50 needed through the sale of his Hub-Gear Triumph. Parting with her would be a sad blow as she had been a reliable old mount and it

would also leave him with no machine to practice on in the months leading up to the race. What little practice he did manage to get was on borrowed machines but these short trips nearly all ended in crashes or mechanical failure. Stanley may have been an inexperienced racer, but he showed early promise as a shrewd negotiator and by the time that entries had closed for the 1922 TT races, everything had been arranged. Cotton would have a machine on the Island for him a few days before the start of practice and they had also agreed to pay half of his entry fee, which was very welcome at the time.

For many weeks leading up to the TT he had not felt at all confident in making a success of his huge undertaking and his only support and encouragement had come from his family and friends.

TT practice was spread over two weeks in the early 1920s and the morning after he arrived on the Isle of Man, Stanley was standing on the pier in Douglas awaiting the arrival of the boat from Liverpool. When the boat docked there was no sign of the Cotton. He met every boat for almost a week and haunted the Steamship Company offices for any information he could find but by Friday he decided not to meet any more boats. Race practice was well under way and another Dublin competitor had loaned him a side-valve Norton, so he decided it was a better use of his time to get some practice in and after the first week his luck began to change. After a full week of practice on the Norton he began to grow in confidence. He was sitting in his hotel lounge after dinner one evening when he heard someone asking for Stanley Woods, at which he jumped up and said: *"I am Stanley Woods."*

His visitor turned out to be the Cotton company team manager and he told him that his machine was outside waiting for him along with the other machines. Stanley went out to find a most decrepit looking motorcycle. It was a bit of a let down as there was no paint or nickel plating on it and the machine looked almost derelict. Harold F Brockbank, who was a well-known sand racer from Southport in Lancashire, and Fred Morgan the Cotton works foreman were standing beside the three machines. After he introduced himself, they pointed out his machine and informed him that it needed some work done to it before he could do any practice on it.

The Cottons had been ridden up from Gloucester to Liverpool. On the way, things had got a little out of hand and the run turned into a bit of a race. An examination of the engine revealed that the exhaust rocker had seized. It was lubricated by the turn of a Grease-cup every 50 miles or so and when it had seized, the inertia of the outside flywheel of the Blackburne engine had sheared the woodruff key locking it to main shaft. Luckily there was no other damage done, the valve was closed when the rocker seized so the piston had not struck the valve. Morgan advised Stanley that he would have to go around to see the Blackburne people and that he would arrange for them to supply him with the necessary parts, but that he would have to fit them himself.

Up to then Stanley had not ridden or even worked on an overhead valve machine, claiming that the nearest he had ever been to one was over the heads of the crowd at Hillberry the previous year, when he watched Howard Davis win the Senior TT. None the less repairing the Cotton turned out to be not such a big job, but to an eighteen-year-old novice, it was quite an undertaking. Stanley spent a sleepless night wondering how things would go the following morning, as riders were not allowed to start their machines on the Promenade, unless they were going to or coming from practice. This meant that after he had made his repairs, he was unable to test the machine, but he need not have worried.

Next morning, he put the machine into gear, opened the throttle a little, and taking advantage of a slight gradient in front of the garage, he attempted to bump-start the engine. The bike fired up immediately, Stanley's supporters and other on-lookers were suitably impressed as he shot up towards the start line for what was to be his first practice.

In the just breaking dawn, he took his place in the line of other racers and it was a great relief to get the signal to start. He made a slow getaway but by the time he had covered three or four miles he was enchanted, for the speed, acceleration and road holding of the Cotton were a revelation.

All seemed well until just below the Highlander when the motor expired. A Norton rider stopped and offered to help. He quickly diagnosed the

problem. The Cotton had been running on a soft spark plug, the rider fixed Stanley up with a race plug and he was off once more. He completed two laps that morning and had no further trouble with the machine.

That evening, just after dinner, the factory representative came into the hotel with another gentleman who he introduced to Stanley as Mr F. Willoughby Cotton. The man asked if he really was Stanley Woods, when Stanley smiled, and replied that he was, Mr Cotton walked out of the room. When Stanley had written to Mr Cotton with his "references," Cotton thought they had signed a potential TT winner. Stanley was clearly a much younger man than they had been expecting, Cotton had wanted a good result in the TT.

There was no telephone connection between the island and the mainland in those days so a telegram had been sent to the Cotton factory to inform them of Stanley's youth and inexperience. By the time the telegram arrived at the works, Mr Cotton had already left for the Island however, so Stanley was able continue practising for a few more sessions. During one morning practice, on the Mountain climb near the East Mountain Gate, the machine seized up. Between pushing and

Norton and Cotton Headquarters, Modwena Hotel in 1922

freewheeling Stanley managed to get the bike back to the workshop.

Fred Morgan got Stanley a replacement piston and cylinder, before he and Harold Brockbank went off to the cinema for the evening. They advised Stanley not to forget to gap the piston rings and re set the tappets to running clearances.

The following morning, he started to run her in carefully and as he made steady progress began to notice aspects of the course, particularly bends and corners that he had not noticed before.

He remembered the valuable advice he had been given by Tommy Greene, an old rider from Dublin who had ridden in the TT just before the Great War and for a few years afterwards and was a first class mechanic.

"No fast laps in practice, learn the course always save your engine as riders who hammer their machines from the start seldom finish."

THOS. E. GREENE – 3½ H.P. RUDGE.
WINNER OF THE GRAND PRIX DE FRANCE, JULY 13TH 1913.

Stanley completed two careful laps that morning and further steady laps the following morning before he felt the new parts were fully run in. Then, he decided to let her go and she went like she never went before, with his next lap time down to 45 minutes, his previous best lap had been 50 minutes. The Junior TT lap record was

THOS. E. GREENE – 3½ H.P. RUDGE.
HOLDER OF THE IRISH END-TO-END RECORD, 400 MILES, 10H-38M APRIL 4TH 1913.

55mph and Stanley knew the machine could go still faster on race day. When practice was over, Mr Cotton called a conference between himself and his riders. He seemed satisfied with the way that things had gone.

On the Monday, the day before the race, all riders had to hand over their machines to be scrutinised by the Auto Cycle Union. After weighing, they were left in a tent in the charge of the A.C.U. until one hour before start time next day.

The Blackburne Company had examined the motor of Stanley's bike a few days before the race. When all the race engines had been previously brake tested at the works, it was this one that was found to give the highest power output. The engine had been ear-marked for another rider, but as the young Woods appeared to have the ability to make good use of the extra power, they decided to leave it with him.

In the early 1920s, the first section of the TT course from the start at Douglas to Ramsey was a bumpy and water-bound road. On dry days when the weather was hot, the clouds of dust made overtaking a hazardous business and intermittent showers made parts of the course very treacherous. It was also full of pot-holes (the section between Sulby and Ramsey being the worst of all) giving riders a hard physical ride on their rigid-framed bikes. The mountain road out of Ramsey was mostly soft sand and loose stone up as far as the Bungalow, with ruts from cart wheels and grass growing between the ruts. The road climbs to just over 1400 feet above sea level at its highest. In those days the Manx Highways Board banned all motor traffic on the mountain section between Ramsey and Creg Ny Baa on the two Sundays prior to race week. The lack of passing vehicles rolling the surface flat probably best explains state of the course on this section. The mountain mist was another problem, though not as much as today due to the relatively low maximum speed of the old racing motorcycles.

Stanley's experience in trials riding had taught him a few things. In particular he had learned to take precautions and check any parts that were likely to vibrate loose. Cottons were delightful machines to ride in his opinion, for the frames were built very low, were rigid and gave a great feeling of security at all times. He found that he could pass faster machines on the mountain because of the Cotton's superior road-holding and found that he could ride either on the crown of the road or in the gutter.

S. WOODS "COTTON"

Upon the resumption of the TT races in 1920, a new class for smaller machines, the Lightweight, had been added to the programme. This class ran concurrently with the Junior TT. There were thirty-two entrants on the smaller machines and the Junior riders had to queue patiently on the grid whilst all the smaller machines were sent off at 30 second intervals. Naturally, being a newcomer, Stanley was very nervous. His race number was 40 so he had a twenty minute wait. When his turn came he moved up to the starting line.

It was when the timekeeper gave him the nod to be on his way that the first of his many troubles occurred. At the weigh-in Stanley had noticed one of the older riders had an extra pocket sewn onto the front of his waistcoat to hold his spare spark plugs. Stanley had liked the idea so he had gone to a local boot maker to have a plug pocket fitted as well. It was not deep enough however, and as he pushed forward, his spare plugs fell out, rattled off the petrol tank and onto the road.

The Cotton had fired up at once, so by the time Stanley had stopped and wheeled her back a bit to retrieve his plugs, his team mate Morgan on machine number 41 was getting way and he had already lost thirty seconds before he had even started. By Quarter Bridge he had caught up with and passed Morgan however.

The two riders that he feared the most had started ahead of him. Howard Davis on his AJS and Cyril Pullin on a Douglas had both drawn earlier start numbers. All the other potential winners were behind him. Approaching Glen Helen he sighted a group of four or five lightweights up ahead and had passed all of them before the top of Creg Willys hill.

His first lap was turning into one of tense enjoyment with his initial nervousness gone; a wisp of dust in the distance might turn into a cloud at the next bend and another machine to be passed. Realising with great satisfaction that some of the machines that he was now overtaking were carrying blue plates, indicating that they were Junior entries (the Lightweight machines carried green plates), he learnt afterwards that he had passed five Juniors and over a dozen Lightweights on the first lap. However, he was becoming a little over-confident, cutting each bend a little closer and leaving the braking a little later. At Governor's Bridge, near the end of the first lap, he decided to try a different approach, but this was not a success, as he ran into the gutter and scraped along the kerb. He did not come off but was both physically and mentally shaken by the incident as he pulled away

from Governor's, accelerating as hard as he could. Speeding past the grandstand and the cheering crowds he got a wave from his pit but it was too early to get any signal as regards his position in the race.

Into his second lap he came across and passed a few more lightweights and about halfway round caught and passed previous TT winner Cyril Pullin on his Douglas. Approaching the 33rd Milestone he caught a glimpse of a group of men standing round the wreckage of a racing motorcycle and a stretcher party carrying off an injured rider. This had a steadying effect and served to remind him to keep things under control.

He found out later that the unlucky rider was a well known Brooklands rider, W. D. Marchant who was riding a Sheffield Henderson. Marchant had originally crashed at Sulby Bridge on the first lap, but had refused all offers of assistance, re-mounted and ridden as far as the 33rd before crashing again. When Marchant recovered after his second spill he had no recollection of his earlier crash.

On his second approach to Governor's Bridge, Stanley was determined not to repeat his first lap mistake, but he did, at about 5 mph faster. Hitting the kerb with a great crash, he was fortunate not to be thrown from the machine. Able to keep going, he headed away from Governor's towards the pits for refuelling, realising that he had damaged his exhaust pipe after hitting the kerb.

Re-fuelling in those days was done using a large can and a funnel rather than the quick fillers used nowadays and riders were permitted to keep their engines running during fill-ups. Stanley's fuel attendant was a bit over enthusiastic and poured a lot of fuel over him and his bike. The spilt fuel was ignited by the flames, which were escaping from where the broken exhaust pipe had parted from the exhaust port. With both the machine and his clothing in flames, he leapt off the machine and attempted to beat out his burning clothes with his gloved hands while backing away from the burning bike. Perhaps he was lucky to trip as he reeled away from the bike, as the pit attendants and race officials present were able to cover him quickly with coats to smother the flames. The fire on the bike was quickly extinguished using Pyrene. As soon as the flames were extinguished there was concern from the officials and Mrs Cotton was heard to shout, *"Stop the boy."* Suggestions were made that he might retire, for the machine looked a bit of a battered wreck by then, but it did not appear to have suffered any material damage. Filling up his tank once more, he pushed off amidst a storm of applause.

Less than two miles into the lap, at Braddan Bridge, the engine suddenly died, for the inlet valve pushrod had broken and had fallen onto the road. This was known to happen and Stanley carried a couple of spare pushrods which were taped to the frame. The only suitable tool was a Lucas "Girder" adjustable spanner which he carried on the front of his belt (he learnt later not to carry it there!) but there was more bad news. The little hardened cap that fitted over the end of the valve had fallen off. A frantic search ensued and the cap was found a few yards away. With great difficulty, managing to compress the valve spring enough to fit the new push rod, he was now on his way once more. Another four miles on, approaching Greeba Castle, the rear brake failed and he found that the corner could be taken a good deal faster than had first thought possible! A quick examination revealed that the rear brake

Leaving Hillberry

cam lever had disintegrated. The front brake was only three inches in diameter - useless, a brake in name only and for the most part, merely symbolic. Off he went again with no thoughts of retiring and just over one hundred miles to go, he would have to keep his speed under control in whatever way he could. Going into the fourth lap, feeling a little tired but full of confidence and approaching Ramsey hairpin, he had forgotten that he had no brakes and approached the bend too fast. He did not even try to negotiate the famous hairpin but went straight on and laid the bike down, speedway fashion, on the loose gravel, the only damage being sustained was a

broken strap on the tool bag. With smaller tools lying all over the road and attempting to gather them up, a Marshal shouted at him *"Never mind your tools keep going, you are doing well!"* With great difficulty, he re-started the motor up hill and got going again, thereafter abusing both his gearbox and the soles of his boots to keep things under control but managing to complete the fourth lap. During the second re-fuelling stop it was suggested to him once again that he should retire but despite all the noise, one of Stanley's friends managed to inform him that he was still in the top six, so it was off again for his last lap of the 1922 Junior TT with his engine still going well.

Described by him many years later as the worst ride that he ever had, his legs were feeling very heavy and a different kind of pain was affecting them, which he thought at the time was fatigue. But he discovered after the race that his upper legs had been scorched, as the cloth breeches he wore offered little protection.

The soles of his boots were worn and tearing away from the welts and uppers and since the incident at Governor's Bridge on the second lap the exhaust had been loose. The exhaust bracket had eventually broken and he had made two stops to re-attach the pipe by tying it in place with a handkerchief. Exhausted after his ordeal, but determined to finish at all costs he succeeding in securing fifth place, finishing twenty-three minutes down on the winning rider, Manxman Tom Sheard

Stanley (Cotton) No 40 Ramsey hairpin crash

With Paddy Johnston and friends

(AJS). If Stanley had not had the serious troubles and the fire, he thought he might have won.

The 1922 Junior TT was unusual compared to preceding years where one make or another was superior to the others and the same make occupied most of the places on the leader board. In the 1922 Junior there were eight different makes of machine in the first ten places.

For the record these were AJS, Sheffield Henderson, Coulson, Cotton, Douglas, Ivy, Edmund and Blackburne.

The 1922 TT had seen the debut of three riders who would go on to make TT history: Stanley Woods - Junior (Cotton), Walter Handley - Lightweight (OK) and Jimmy Simpson - Senior (Scott). Between them they won fifteen TT races, made twenty-eight fastest laps, with Stanley taking eleven, Handley nine and Simpson eight. Walter switched to car racing some years before the outbreak of World War Two. He was a pilot and was killed in an air crash in 1941, whilst serving with the Air Transport Auxiliary. Jimmy Simpson who was the first to set 60, 70 and 80 mph laps in a TT race, retired from racing at the end of the 1934 to take up a job with Shell BP.

The Nesbit Shield

This trophy was awarded at the TT in commemoration of Mr J.R. Nesbit who had been the chairman of the Auto-Cycle Union for many years. This prize, to quote the Official Programme, might be awarded at the discretion of the Stewards, "to the rider or riders who exhibit such pluck and endurance or such capacity to triumph over difficulties as to deserve special recognition." Most people thought that this trophy should have been awarded to the young Stanley in 1922 for his sheer dogged determination. The ensuing controversy when he did not receive it was great publicity for Woods and also for Cotton, who saw a six-fold increase in sales of their machines.

After the TT several riders made for the Continent, including Walter Handley and Stanley, who were to ride

Walter Handley (OK Junior)

Stanley posing with Silver Replica

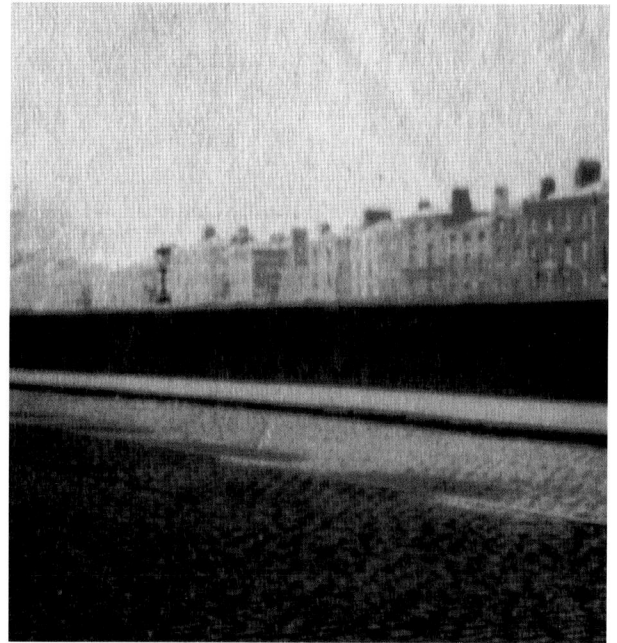

26/28th June 1922 Artillery shells explode over The Four Courts Dublin as Irish Free State Troops open fire to dislodge anti-treaty forces, over 100 taken prisoner Considerable damage to surrounding buildings.

Troubled times in Ireland - Rathfarnham Barracks (three photos above taken by Stanley with his box Brownie camera)

for Ernie Humphries on OK Juniors in the 250cc classes at the "Grand Prix" and the Belgian GP. The French GP was considered so important at that time that it was known simply as the "Grand Prix." It was run on Wednesday July 12th on public roads south of Strasbourg in eastern France and the same circuit was also used for the car GP (Strasbourg had just been liberated after the First World War). The TT winners Alec Bennett and Geoff Davison repeated their success in the Senior and Lightweight events respectively. Woods had to retire with a broken valve – at the time probably the most frequent cause for retirements through mechanical misfortune.

The Belgian GP was held at Spa on Sunday 23rd July. A thunderstorm broke just before the start of the race. G.S Davison completed a "Hat Trick" by winning the 250 class on a Levis. His time was just over four and a quarter hours and this was in drenching rain. Walter Handley was the only other finisher in the 250 class, several minutes behind Davison. Stanley retired with a wet magneto.

Back home Stanley raced at the Temple 50 on the following Saturday riding a 350cc Cotton, retired on lap eight but won at Portmarnock the next day on the same machine.

ULSTER GRAND PRIX

The first UGP was held on 14th October 1922, run on the twenty and a half mile Clady circuit as a handicap race but with scratch winners. Moving spirits in persuading the Northern Ireland Government of the time to enact legislation allowing roads to be closed for motor sport events were Harry Ferguson (famous inventor and engineer) and William J Chambers, two of the major men behind the first Prix.

Harry Ferguson   *William Chambers*

The race attracted a large enthusiastic crowd but although his name appears in the programme, Stanley did not ride. An old aunt of his had died in tragic circumstances and, mourning being what it was in those days, he was not permitted to take part. However, he had learned a lot from the 1922 season and had gone from being "just another rider" to one tipped as a future winner.

1923

1923 was a momentous year for young Stanley Woods. Having ridden in the previous year's TT, his ambition was to become a racing motorcyclist and to win the greatest of all races, the Tourist Trophy. His aim was to be included in the Cotton team for the second year and to have the use of a machine for selected events in Ireland as well. His first race in 1923 was on April 21st in County Down at the Ulster Motorcycle Club's "*Clandeboye 50*" where he rode the 350 Cotton, this ended in retirement but with fastest lap. The winning rider was Noel Metcalf on a Brough Superior with Herbie Chambers, the runner-up on a 350 AJS.

Norton and Cotton Headquarter Modwena Hotel

Most of May was taken up with preparation for the TT and he knew how important it was to be 100% fit for this great event. Having tried his machine in practice, against those machines considered to be the main opposition, he entered the Junior race in a confident mood. He was also entered in the Lightweight race as this was to be run separately for the first time and together with the Junior was increased to six laps.

He had been careful planning not to use full throttle until the final lap if he was still in the running. The first two laps were uneventful but he found, for the first time, that the machine had the habit of jumping out of top gear. This necessitated holding the gear lever in place for most of the race.

After the race was over an examination revealed that the gear control rod had got bent which had most likely happened just before or just after the weigh-in.

Scrutineering

Cotton garage

Practise day

Signing on

With the model running well however and confident in his own riding ability, he knew he must be doing well, but he also knew that he had to resist the temptation to take any undue risks or to overstress the motor.

Having settled reasonably well into the race, he made a fuel stop at the end of his second lap, where his pit attendant told him that he had been in fifth position at the end of the first lap and half a minute down on Jimmy Simpson who had lapped at almost 60 mph. Jimmy's lap of 38 minutes from a standing start was more than two minutes faster than the old record.

To put this tremendous performance into perspective, it has to be remembered that this was only Jimmy's second year at the TT. In between Simpson and Stanley were Charlie Hough (AJS), Bert Le Vack (New Imperial) and Tommy de la Hay on a Sunbeam.

For his third lap Stanley decided to keep things under control and to try to maintain the speed he had been doing. He felt that the leaders could not possibly maintain the pace they were setting and that he should play a waiting game and wait for them to drop out. At the end of the third lap, still going well, he was signalled

Governors Bridge

as lying third, so his hunch was right and the faster men were dropping out as he had anticipated. Completing another lap at much the same speed before stopping for fuel for the final time, he learned that he had been in second place behind Bert Le Vack at the end of the previous circuit. Despite being very fit, and having undergone special training, Stanley began to find the going very tiring, particularly on the section between Sulby and Ramsey.

The frame of the Cotton was longer in the wheelbase than the previous year's model and did not steer as well. He felt so bad he advised his pit attendant that he did not think he could go the distance: the pit man observed that Le Vack was slowing a little. His start number was 28 and Woods was number 29. To try to make up the thirty seconds that Le Vack had started ahead of him, Stanley had to abandon his cautious tactics and it was full throttle from the start of the fifth lap.

Mile after mile was covered looking for the tell-tale cloud of dust from his rival but by now he had either forgotten or become accustomed to the fatigue that had dogged him earlier on. At Sulby, a lonely rider standing by his machine gave him a hearty wave; it was No. 28, Bert le Vack. Getting a wave from one of his heroes with only a lap and half to go, had the wrong effect on him. The correct thing to do would have been to ease off on his previous speed. Instead he went faster.

Entering Parliament Square in Ramsey, he ran wide and hit the footpath on the far side. He managed to stay on board but ended up in someone's back door, the front forks were bent back and the front mudguard was fouling the exhaust pipe. He kicked the mudguard clear of the exhaust and was on his way once more. This had unfortunately cost him three minutes and also the lead, as George Dance had passed him during his stop. The machine's bent forks handicapped Stanley. The steering was impaired so he had to slow down on corners.

As mentioned, the race distance for the Junior TT had been extended to six laps for the first time, and going into the final lap still in second place, his pit crew signalled him to go faster. This he did, the engine was still running smoothly and revving freely, but his cornering speed was much slower than it had been.

The incident at Ramsey had given Dance a great lead. He had been in third place going into the fourth lap, and could have afforded to slow a little but as he was carrying an early start number he was unaware of this and continued to drive hard. His engine broke an exhaust valve just before the Bungalow and was forced to retire only ten miles from the finish, leaving Stanley to win by nearly three minutes.

Words cannot describe the scenes with crowds of well-wishers greeting him at the finish and at his hotel later that evening. When it was time for him to go to The Palace for the presentation, he was carried shoulder high by his supporters.

He had little respite because the Lightweight race was the following day. He was never in contention however

S. WOODS "COTTON" WINNER OF JUNIOR T.T. RACE 1923

Smiling 1923 Junior TT Winner

JUNIOR T.T.
WON
by S. Woods on a Cotton
fitted with

Blackburne
Engine.

Burney & Blackburne Ltd., Atlas Works, Bookham.
SURREY.

'Phone : Bookham 44.   Telegrams : "ENGINES."

Reception at Kingston

and retired early on in the race due to engine trouble. Jock Porter on his self-built New Gerard won the race. (This was not the first or last time that a motorcycle manufacturer personally competed successfully in such a motorcycle marathon). For the second year in a row the fastest lap in the Lightweight race went to Walter Handley. That afternoon the Auto Cycle Union staged the inaugural running of the Sidecar TT. The legendary Freddie Dixon (Douglas) won the race after a hectic battle with Harry Langman (Scott) who had taken the lead on the second lap but then crashed at Braddan Bridge.

In the Senior race, run in drizzling rain, Stanley took over Harry Langman's entry but had no further success, for the Scott expired on the first lap.

A TT win was world-wide news in those days, even though it might have taken rather longer to get to its remoter corners than with today's technology.

However, the news had definitely reached Dublin and, fittingly, Stanley was met from the boat by the Lord Mayor and given a motorcycle escort into Dublin, where he arrived to the adulation of his family, friends and the media. In just two years he had gone from novice motorcyclist sitting on the verge at Hillberry, to becoming an accomplished racer and the hero of his nation.

To emphasise his achievement, just consider the words of one seasoned onlooker, a reporter for The Motor Cycle who described Stanley's progress through that same un-surfaced Hillberry corner on his 1923 winning ride with:

"The sliding wheels of Woods's Cotton threw up a bow-wave of dirt and stone from his wheels. All through this giant slide, at perhaps 60 mph, he was rock steady, master of his machine and himself."

WON THE 1923 I.O.M. JUNIOR T.T. ON A COTTON

STANLEY WOODS. (IRELAND) Winner of 10 Isle of Man Tourist Trophy Races. 1923, '26, '32 '33, '35, '38, '39.

by Jock Leyden

With F.W. Cotton (wearing bow tie)

The Leinster 100 held on 14th July was the first ever official road race in the Irish Free State. Organised by the Leinster Motorcycle & Light Car Club, it was run on an eleven mile road circuit starting near the village of Dunshaughlin Co. Meath.

Noel Medcalf (Brough Superior) won the handicap, Graham Walker (Norton) was second

Finishers Gold Medal

and made fastest time with Stanley Woods (Cotton) third. To explain just how good the Irish handicappers were, the first six finishers with their models ranging from 249cc to 976cc finished within 60 seconds of the winner.

In the second Ulster Grand Prix in 1923, starting from Denny Loan School on the Clady Straight, Stanley Woods in his first UGP, had to call it a day when an engine bolt fouled the outside flywheel of his Cotton Blackburne.

Refuelling at the Leinster 100

Stanley with supporters

1924 STANLEY'S WORDS

"On the Thursday of UGP week, I had ridden up from Dublin with my future brother-in-law, Gordon Burney and a couple of friends. There was no official practice in the early days; we came out around the course for some unofficial practicing. The local constabulary was very kind and looked the other way mostly. We stopped somewhere along the Clady Straight to effect some repair or adjustment. A woman came out of her house, a farmer's wife I assume and invited us all in. We were treated to boiled eggs, scones, tea, you name it. It must have been for us the highlight of the meeting. However, in the race itself, I was riding a 1000cc side-valve New Imperial JAP. This machine had a maximum speed of about 95mph and was very considerably faster than any of the 500s. In actual fact they ran a 600cc. class in those days.

I was quite confident that I would win the race. Unfortunately, I had petrol tank trouble and right from the beginning I was in serious trouble. Joe Craig won the 600cc class on a Norton. I won the 1000cc race on the New Imperial at a lower speed than the 250s. I had bought the big 1000cc machine because I thought that the 350 Cotton that I had won the 1923 TT on as somewhat of a toy. I had been used to a Harley Davidson solo and sidecar, and this is how this big four cam JAP-engined machine had evolved.

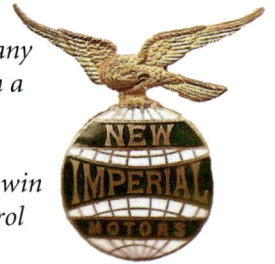

Gordon Burney, Leinster 100 start

Burney at speed

William Cosgrove (First Taoiseach) with winner Gordon Burney

The Tailteann Games, 1924 Sidecar Event

Dene Allen (Norton) and passenger, winner of the Sidecar Event in the Tailteann Games of 1924.

New Imperial

Joe Craig (Norton) winner 600 Class Note: Northern Ireland registrations

I actually went to the motorcycle show at Olympia in 1923 with the idea of purchasing a Brough Superior SS80. This appeared to me, on paper, to be the most suitable motorcycle maker fitting the big JAP engine. However, I was looking for a discount off the machine. I had just won the Junior TT and had a big head. George Brough was not interested. I ferreted around the rest of the show and looked at Coventry Eagle and Zenith. I finally set my eye on a New Imperial. Norman Downs, founder and managing director of New Imperial Motors, was a very keen supporter of the TT.

When I approached him he was prepared to co-operate one hundred percent. 'Go and see the JAP people, the gearbox, the carburettor, the magneto people and whatever they will do for you, we will do the same.' I got a machine at about 40% off instead of the normal trade 20%. It turned out to be a fabulous machine.

I entered it in a couple of road races in Northern Ireland, the Temple and the Cookstown Hundreds. I soon learned that this machine was quite unsuitable to these small local races. However, I had a very successful season south of the border, sand races, and a road race in the Phoenix Park, sprints and all that sort of thing. Towards the end of the season, J.A. Prestwich introduced an OHV version of this big twin and again the Brough seemed to be the best thing. Again, George was not

interested. He was prepared to sell me one but not at a discount, despite the fact that I had won virtually all the Irish Championships in the previous year. I did not like any of the other machines at the show.

I went to New Imperial and they said that they were not fitting the overhead valve engine. It would not fit into their frame. I explained to them that if they altered the frame somewhat, "modifications to the upper frame and steering head assembly". This they agreed to do and fit an OHV engine. I had a little trouble with the steering on the side-valve machine.

Every now and again she would wriggle her head at me, a bit like the early Norton with Druid forks. I drew my own conclusions and went to Webbs who produced for me a set of heavyweight forks for this one off machine, which steered to perfection. In view of the tank trouble that I had, I got a pair of pannier tanks and soldered and riveted them together and that solved that trouble.

Cookstown 70

the cracked shell. In the meantime, I had sent a telegram to Sturmey-Archer, to send a gearbox shell to Belfast.

I did not enter her in any road races except the Leinster 100 and the Ulster Grand Prix. I was also pulling a sidecar, a light affair, in other events. I had the machine all ready to come up to Ulster, probably the Tuesday or Wednesday of race week. As I was leaving the garage where I was friendly with the proprietor and his foreman and had a lockup garage in his yard. I demonstrated a flamboyant display of acceleration away from the garage and I am afraid that I pushed the back out of the gearbox. It was not strong enough to take the power. I had to ride to Belfast on top gear only, stopping every fifty miles or so or even more, to put in a mixture of grease and oil that was coming out of

The post was pretty good in those days. The gearbox shell arrived on mid-day Friday. I had no practice on the Friday. I think that I got the machine ready for the race at about 11 o'clock that night. Next morning, I came out to the race full of hope and took off like a shot out of a gun in front of thousands. I was in trouble immediately because I was too exuberant. I was enjoying every bump and humpback.

Now I am not quite sure what happened on the first lap but something delayed me and could not say on which lap the various troubles came along. I had to remove the rear mudguard and carry on and had to stop virtually on every lap and hammer the dents out of the front mudguard.

Transport during TT Week

Four of the class winners – Joe Craig Jimmy Shaw Stanley Woods & Gordon Burney with the Ulster Prime Minister Sir James Craig

Jimmy Shaw No 61 winner of the Unlimited Handicap

Everything was bottoming out. I had no sense because I kept using full throttle over the bumps. I could easily have made best time of the day if I had taken it a bit easier but I learned from my mistakes but I was full of the joy of spring and had won the race for the second year.

Incidentally, also I forgot to mention that in 1924 I took the side-valve twin to the Isle of Man as a hack machine. Cottons were in dreadful trouble that year. I don't know how it came about but they were not a very precision-built machine and somewhere along the line they went wrong in the frame. The race frame was slightly different from the standard frame, but they made the frames, or allegedly made the frames on the same jigs and used the same engine plates and were starting to pull the back lugs out of the crankcases. We had to fabricate new engine plates from sheet steel in order to overcome the trouble.

On one of the mornings, when my machine was laid up, I put my Junior numbers on the big New Imperial to go out and impress the boys. I got as far as Ballacraine alright but from Ballacraine to Glen Helen I realised the error of my ways. A big, heavy bike travelling probably 10 or 15mph faster than I was used to on a 350, proved somewhat of a handful. I did not lose it. I eased her back a bit and I cruised home with my tail between my legs and that's the first time that I ever told that little tale, in public."

He rode for Cotton using the same machine in the Senior and Junior TTs of 1924, retired in both, one of these rides being probably the shortest race on record as he did not get beyond the pits.

1925

Stanley had been working for his father up until this time, ten shillings a week plus running costs and plenty of time off. He competed in many smaller Irish Road Races such as the Cookstown 100, Temple 50, Athy 75, Leinster 100, Carrowdore 100 and also the Phoenix Park. These marvellous races were run on a handicap basis and he was almost always the Scratch-man, giving all the others a start. He only won a few, but if 'First Places' in the lesser Irish Road handicaps eluded him, 'Fastest Time' awards came thick and fast. He had the ability to memorize a road race course from the briefest possible experience of it and ride as if he had been living there for weeks.

In addition to his road racing he tackled sand racing, with the beaches of Magilligan Strands Co. Derry being 'happy hunting grounds.' They were approximately 170 miles from Dublin and the average distance of the races was 100 miles. This meant that between the time that he left his home in Rathmines, situated on the south side of Dublin and climbed into bed late that night, he had put some 500 miles of road and sand behind him. He must have been well known to the Customs Officers at the Irish Boundary, but how he was able to cross the border so late in the evening is one of those things that nobody knows, as the New Imperial had no lights.

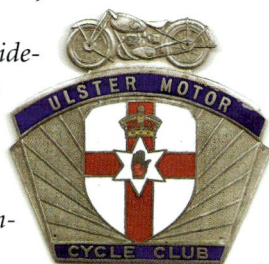

Stanley was also a leading figure in Trials, Side-car racing with his great rival Dene Allen (the Norton agent in Dublin), Charlie Manders (Sunbeam) and George Briggs (Montgomery-JAP) in the Phoenix Park and Portmarnock Sand Races. A recurrent winner of sprints, he held many course records and for a long period, was one of Ireland's best Grass-track performers, with over one hundred awards.

British Customs Post, Newry

Beach racing

Herbie Chambers (AJS) Portmarnock Strand September 1925 sadly he lost his life that day

STANLEY'S WORDS

"*I did ride at Brooklands on a couple of occasions - no successes however. In 1925 Gordon Burney & I entered for a The Two Hundred Mile. I don't know what happened to him but I sent my machine to J.A.P.'s to be to be prepared. It was the New Imperial 1000 cc OHV JAP as ridden by me in the Ulster that year.*

When they saw it they would not let me ride it, as according to them it was unrideable at Brooklands and they changed my entry to a Zenith. I cannot remember what happened to it or me in the race – it was, in my opinion completely unmanageable (I think that the petrol tank burst early in the race). I was convinced always that I could have done really well on the New Imperial as it steered as the Norton did in the years that followed."

Stanley pulled up on his 31st lap, fuel streaming out of the front of his huge tank and retired. This was how The Motor Cycle related it.

1925 TT

1924 & 1925 were barren years as far as the TT was concerned: he rode a New Imperial - JAP in the Lightweight but ended in retirement.

The Enfield Cycle Co had offered him £100 to ride one of their machines in the Junior, not bad money in those days.

He said it was a lovely little bike, but not very fast. Whilst lying fifth, he crashed at Ballig Bridge, on the last lap and the handlebar broke on the right hand side, so he moved the throttle control over to the left side of the remaining bar and carried on. The nearest Marshalling Post tried to stop him, but failed. They phoned ahead

Stanley wearing his flying helmet with Gordon (Royal Enfields) at start of Reliability trial

Gordon and Stanley, official Royal Enfield entries

and Marshals managed to stop him at 'The Bungalow' with only 10 miles to go. He was not very happy! For your handlebar to break in a race is once in a lifetime experience, but when added to his Harley Davidson escapade, it meant it had happened to him twice!

Norton Motors had won the Senior and Sidecar Races the previous year, their first since 1907. They had by then some older riders and were looking for some new blood. Bill Mansell and Walter Moore used to go out at practice to watch proceedings. Stanley knew that they were out there, but never knew where, so he could

Stanley, Gordon and Ted with Vauxhall car

not put on a show; however, they spotted his riding and offered him a job.

They had a vacancy with their outside travelling staff at £4 per week and an offer to ride for them in the 1926 Senior TT. At first he turned them down, as he was by then working full time with Mackintosh's at £6.10 shillings per week salary, the use of a company car seven days a week plus expenses.

With only two weeks off for holidays, time off for racing was a problem. In Ireland things began to turn sour, for the great post-war depression was just beginning to bite everywhere. Stanley and his father had done very good business in what had been former 'Garrison Towns' in Ireland, but the British Army and their families had now left and trade had followed the flag.

At the Olympia Motorcycle Show Stanley's friend Dene Allen met up with Bill Mansell and suggested that they should consider adding another Irishman to their team; they already had three Ulster-born riders, Alec Bennett, Joe Craig and Jimmy Shaw.

As a result, Stanley was invited to Birmingham late in the year and it was agreed that he would ride for Norton in the Senior TT. They would send him over a Model 18, a standard O.H.V. sports machine, for everyday use and to compete in all sorts of Irish Motorcycling events, as they were keen on any publicity.

Joe Craig Senior T.T. 1925.

CHAPTER FOUR

1926-1930

1926

IT WAS ON this very machine that Stanley notched up his first Norton victory in February 1926 by winning Ireland's premier trial, the Leinster Motorcycle Club's Patland Cup Trial.

Showing his versatility, at a hill-climb at Ballinascorney Gap in May, run by the Dublin University Motorcycle Club, Stanley made fastest time in both solo (Norton) and side-car (New Imperial twin) classes.

Stanley took the Norton to the Island early and got a few days useful practice before the team arrived. The Race Machines were even better. Superficially, they appeared like Model 18s but they were very different. Forks were special heavyweight Webbs, front brake was an eight inch Enfield and the engine embodied an improved dry-sump oil pump (better than the 1925 TT version), while racing cams giving substantially longer dwell than the standard Model 18 versions. In addition, the mainshafts of the engine were increased in size to 1" diameter and steel flywheels were employed. Large oil tanks were fitted as well as large capacity pannier fuel tanks. Careful assembly from selected parts and everything well harmonized made for a very potent machine.

All went well in practice, until the con-rod broke. When an engine fails in this way it often means that pieces of metal are circulating with the oil, so the oil-pump has to be stripped out and all the oil-ways blown

A Bennet (Velocette) winner Junior TT 1926

P Ghersi consoled by C W Johnston after Lightweight TT

clear. Of course, the flywheels have to be taken out of the crankcase and parted for the new con-rod, big-end etc. to be fitted. After the engine was stripped and rebuilt it just would not rev although Walter Moore said that it had been rebuilt just as it originally had been. Moore stripped the engine once more after practice had finished and claimed that he had found the trouble - that the crankshaft was out of line. Stanley said, none the less, that it was never as good as the original engine.

The outstanding happening of the year was the triple Irish victory in the TT events. Alec Bennett riding the relatively new Velocette overhead camshaft machine won the Junior at record speed, the first TT win by an overhead camshaft engine. Veloce of Birmingham, was a small family owned, world renowned manufacturer of quality motorcycles and famous for their development of O.H.C. racing engines.

Paddy Johnson won the Lightweight (now increased to seven laps) and headed a Cotton hat-trick. This was the first and only time in TT history that a machine with a proprietary engine took the first three places.

The Lightweight was also noteworthy for the appearance of the Italian marque Moto Guzzi - a name that was to feature strongly in Stanley's later racing career. By 1926 they were a leading marque, even outside Italy, and had great hopes of victory in the Lightweight TT. Pietro Ghersi from Genoa was riding their new S.O.H.C. 250. This had a rather advanced specification, low weight distribution, was easy to handle, fast and comparatively reliable. Ghersi, after posting a new class record, came in to refill at the end of the third lap and requested a plug change as well. After the race, the stewards announced that it was with great regret they had to disqualify No 16, Pietro Ghersi, from the results, for a breach of the regulations involving the use of a spark plug which was not in accordance with the make declared on the entry form. However, he was allowed to keep the new lap record, as it was achieved on the original plug.

Moving on to the third Irish victory of 1926, the Senior TT was run in good weather. Woods was the junior member of the "Norton Works Runners," but that did not worry him, for he was young and full of enthusiasm. Jimmy Simpson (AJS) made his usual 'Meteoric Start' and raised the course record to over 70mph (70.43), leading for over two laps before his engine gave up. Woods then took the lead but was chased by Charlie Hough on another AJS, who was employed by A J Stevens, 39 seconds

Stanley pushing off, Senior TT

Parliament Square, Ramsey

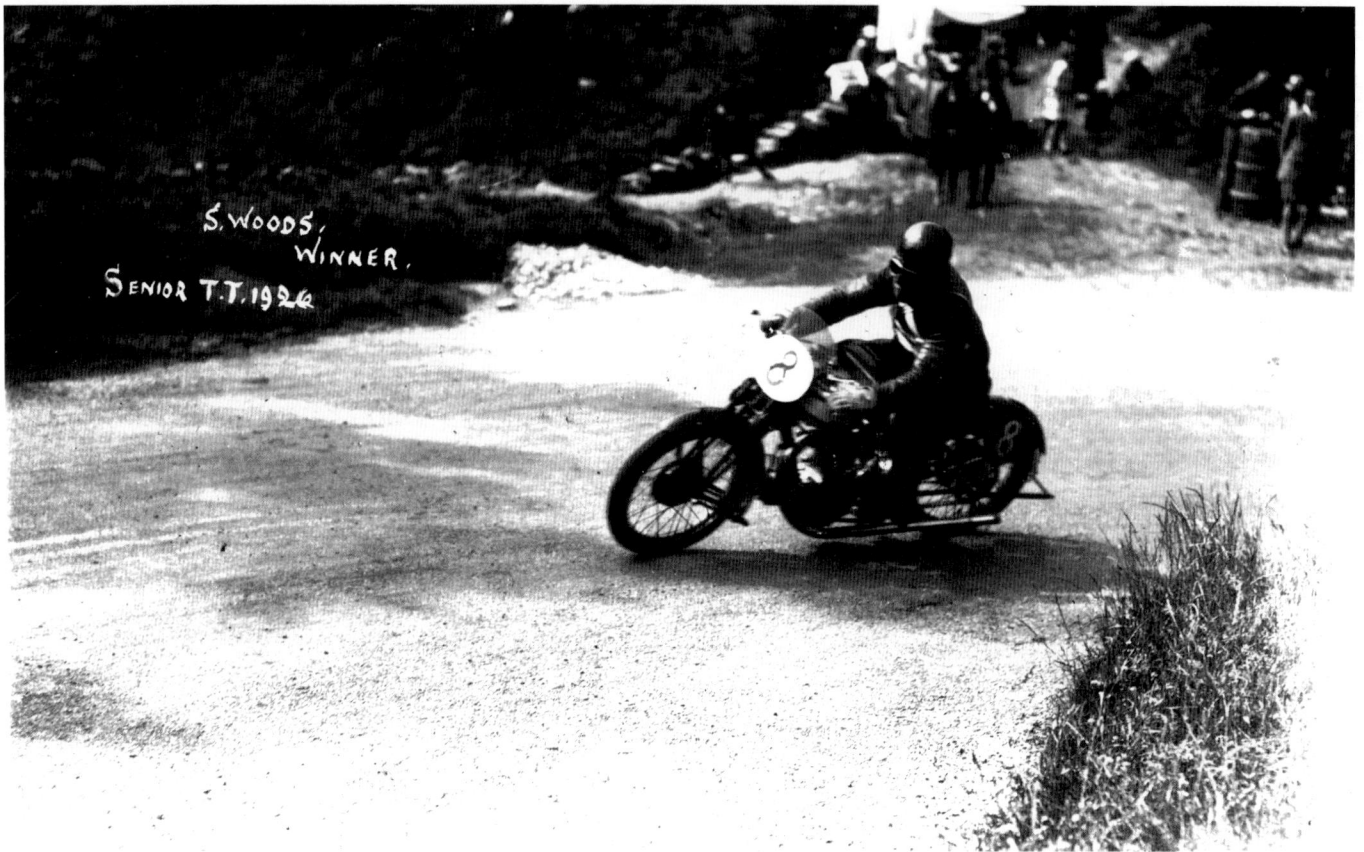

S. WOODS,
WINNER,
SENIOR T.T. 1926

Ramsey Hairpin

K.E. 965 VALVES

Senior TT Winner

Stanley and Walter Handley, 1st and 2nd, 1926 Senior TT

in arrears. But Hough crashed on the last lap near Ramsey.

The result was an impressive victory for Stanley Woods, at record speed on his Norton debut, despite the A.C.U.'s insistence on the use of commercial fuel, rather than the alcohol previously allowed. Walter Handley (Rex Acme) was second after a plug change, with Frank Longman, (AJS), third.

STANLEY'S WORDS
"After the TT it was off to the Belgian GP: that year it was the Grand Prix of Europe. I led the Belgian from the start on a 500 Norton until about three quarter distance when I got a puncture in the front tyre. I rode about half a lap flat and changed a wheel complete. I lost a lot of time and could not get the brake cable connected but put up a new record lap later, in fact quite a number of them and finished third."

"I had no luck in the Ulster Grand Prix - I think that I was leading on the Norton and retired. I gave out to the Press that my 'Tail light had gone out,' one never really blamed what did happen. What actually happened was

that the front down tube on the frame broke below the steering-head, somewhere along the Clady Straight. This had been known to happen before and we used to lead the HT lead from the magneto, which was in front of the engine, up through the sidecar lug, which was under the petrol tank at the front and on to the spark plug, so when the frame broke and the gap opened, it pulled the lead out of the magneto and all was well, nobody crashed."

Stanley had suddenly discovered his engine rubbing the road, the 'open frame' of his Norton having broken at the head at 90 mph on the Clady straight …

STANLEY'S WORDS
"I turned professional with Nortons; I managed three weeks on the Island, plus two weeks (almost) for the Belgian, which I extended somewhat on my way home to visit the 'current girl-friend' on the Isle of Man. I think that it must have been about three weeks in all. I was supposed to be at home resting a damaged ankle after falling off the big 1000cc OHV New Imperial in the Phoenix Park. Then another week for the 'Ulster', but by then I had given in my resignation to Mackintosh. I was

1926.

Senior I.O.M. T.T.   1st

Norton Motors.	£ 500	· 0 · 0
First Prize.	20	· 0 · 0
K.L.G. Plugs.	500	· 0 · 0
Coventry Chains	50	· 0 · 0
Sturmey Archer	50	· 0 · 0
John Bull	6	· 6 · 0
Wellworthy Rings	10	· 0 · 0
B. & B. Carburetters	30	· 0 · 0
Castrol Oil	150	· 0 · 0
'B.P.' Petrol	50	· 0 · 0
'Mosley'	10	· 10 · 0
Dunlop	200	· 0 · 0
Webb Forks	5	· 0 · 0
Feelemit	10	· 0 · 0
C.A.V. Magnetos	25	· 0 · 0
Norton Personal.	15	· 0 · 0
£	1631	· 16 · 0

preparing to join Norton full time, plus from late 1927, started my own Toffee Factory, 'TT Toffee.' Regarding English trials, I did not ride in very many.

The Scott was my favourite: in 1926 I finished to win a first class award, then did not compete again until, I think 1931, when I made fastest time and was placed 2nd on

Irish Customs Post

Travelling to UGP

Scott Trial Yorkshire

Present from Club

Rucca Club badge

Time and Observation on a Camshaft Norton that I used for trials, scrambles, road, grass, sand racing and sidecar. A real friend, this machine was first issued by the Works to Jimmy Guthrie early in 1928 but I had it from October 1928 until I left Norton in the winter of 1933."

The Dublin and District MCC, Donabate Speed Trials, August 1926 would be the last time the enthusiasts would see Woods astride the New Imperial twin in competition, for it would now be sold as he was off to Birmingham to

take up his appointment with Nortons after the Ulster Grand Prix.

At the Donabate Speed Trials, Woods provided Saturday afternoon sensations by setting records in three events. First, the Half-mile, with a flying start on the 986cc New Imperial, 17.15 secs (104.7 mph). Then on a 490 Norton he won the under 600cc solo class from scratch at 88.36 mph, and finally, on the same machine with side-car, won the Unlimited Side-car Handicap at 81.08 mph. Quite a good afternoon!

1927

In early 1927, he had exchanged his previous company car for a Norton and sidecar to cover his run as their representative, mostly in the north of England. One customer that he did call on was Dan Bradbury of Sheffield. Stanley got quite friendly with Dan's daughter. Dan was a Norton and Velocette agent and was one of a very few Velocette shareholders outside of the Goodman family.

During this time Stanley also worked at the experimental department with Walter Moore on the preparation of the racing engines. In addition, he worked as a tester for a while with the new 'cradle frames,' sometimes riding as far as Southampton and back in a day.

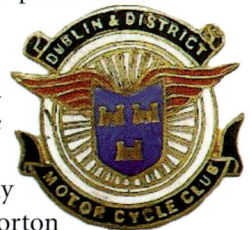

Dan Bradbury Promotional Ashtray

FIRST OUTING FOR THE CAMSHAFT NORTON

It was known that Walter Moore had been working on a new Overhead Camshaft engine in readiness for the TT. To save costs much of the bottom half of the engine was similar to the 1926 TT jobs and the famous 79x100mm bore and stroke were retained. It was decided to enter two machines in Germany where preliminary tests could be carried out.

This was the first race for the new Norton (now with cradle frame) on May 22nd at the 'Rund um die Solitude' near Stuttgart. Five 'Classes' were put together for the main race, the classes starting at two minute intervals, eight laps for the 175 cc and 250 cc capacity classes and a ten lap race for the larger machines.

There were a total of 81 starters with two Irish riders starting in the Half Litre class, TT winner Stanley Woods and Joe Craig. The Kassel Daily News on the 23rd of May reported that Woods was by far the fastest, leading until his engine overheated on the eighth lap, when he had to retire.

BLIND FLYING

Before 1927, Stanley considered that practising on a really bad morning at the TT was a waste of time, so he evolved a system he called 'Blind Flying.' Choosing a section at a time, he rode back and forth, when necessary with the aid of friends to

signal him. In this way, he gained an intimate knowledge of the course by practising under all conditions and doing as many laps as he could every morning. He learnt and memorised the sequence of the bends and corners, whilst noting landmarks for 'misty riding.' He knew that unless a feature was reasonably prominent it would be too difficult to locate when visibility was poor or possibly be obscured by spectators on race day. Finding the edge of the road, following the grass banks to navigate through the mist, walls, trees, and telegraph poles - all could be used as indicators of the road ahead; consequently he could speed through the mist with only the slightest reduction in speed.

1927 TT

During practice for the 1927 TT Archie Birkin, only twenty-one years of age, a brother of Tim Birkin (who made racing history in his Bentleys), crashed and was killed when he swerved to avoid a vehicle coming in the opposite direction just outside the village of Kirkmichael (now known as Birkin's Bend). As the roads were open to ordinary traffic, the early runners in practice were taking their lives in their hands and that incident led to the roads being closed for practice from 1928.

For the 1927 TT, Nortons ran not only the new Camshaft machines but also OHV machines which utilized the same frame and other parts – the fore-runner of the ES2 model which appeared later that year at the Olympia Show.

On the evening before the Senior TT, team mate Bennett remarked to Stanley: "*Well, do you think you are*

Shaw, Stanley, and engine designer Walter Moore
congratulate winner Bennett

going to win tomorrow?" His reply was: *"While I am going, I will be ahead of you."* Alec smiled and said: *"Time will tell."*

In the event, Stanley got off to a fast start and led second man Bennett by a minute per lap. After three laps Woods came in to refuel; his only pit instructions were: *"Keep going as you are."*

He kept going to the extent that on the fifth lap, with a five minute lead, the tongues on the central body of the clutch sheared, just past Ginger Hall and he was forced to retire.

Stanley, of course, should have won. He could have eased off a bit because up until the fourth lap he was leading second man Bennett by an ever increasing number of seconds per lap, but was not aware of his position until after the race. Bennett's winning average was 68.41 mph, from Jimmy Guthrie (New Hudson) with Tommy Simister (Triumph) third. Jimmy Shaw, on one of the new OHV cradle framed Nortons, was fourth.

Jimmy Guthrie, a motor mechanic from Hawick, Scotland was a late-comer to the TT. He was born in 1897 and made his debut in the 1923 Junior TT during which he retired. He was virtually unknown from then until his return in 1927. Over the next ten years Stanley and Guthrie would become great friends as well as rivals.

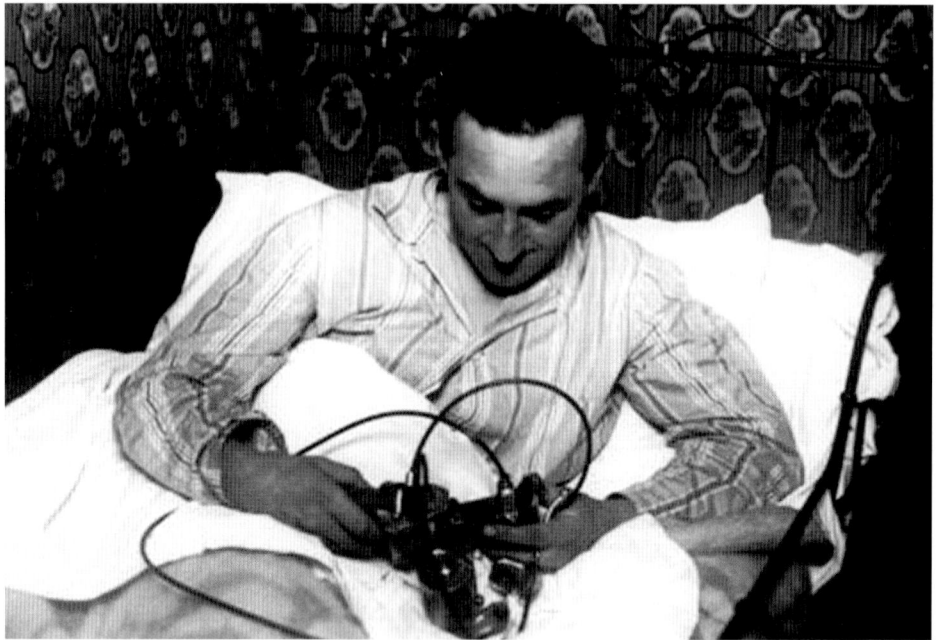

Night before the Assen race

Stanley was a thinking rider and you will read several references here on how he would nurse his engine during the early stages of a race, before indulging in full throttle.

He explained his tactic with: *"When I started racing in the early 1920s it was an accepted fact that whoever led in the early stages of a race did not win, or finish for that matter. Usually it was engine trouble that put an end to a meteoric start, but not one component part of machines of those days could be described as beyond suspicion."*

Engines did slowly become more reliable, but in a long race like the TT they were under tremendous stress and Stanley always treated them with care. His experiences in the 1927 TT taught him two lessons. First, he would need to find a workable signalling system, so that he could control his own race pace, for there had to be a better method than the one in use. Secondly, he learned not only to keep an eye on what the opposition were doing, but also his own team.

Going back to his problem in the 1927 Senior, the engine designer Walter Moore, as Stanley found out later, had advised Bennett that after every practice session always to have

Norton pit, Assen TT

Stanley winner of the 500 Class of the First Dutch International TT

events: the very first international Dutch TT, by five minutes; then, the Swiss GP by three minutes at an average speed quicker than the previous lap record (chased home by Freddie Dixon (HRD).

At the Belgian GP circuit at Spa Francorchamps, which had just been surfaced with tar, Stanley won at an average of 71.7 mph, (the first time that the 70 mph barrier had been broken), twenty-two minutes ahead of Ernie Nott (Rudge).

The 1927 German Grand Prix was held at the newly opened Nurburgring in the Eifel Mountains, during the Grand Prix of Europe. The Blue Riband 500c.c. Class was run on the 3rd July while the other classes were run on the previous day. With something like one hundred and seventy bends, the course was seventeen miles long and, for the 500s, the race itself was just over three hundred miles long. The course winds in and out of bends and up and down hills, the only chance for a burst of speed being the mile and a half to the finish and the grandstand (which was 1500 ft above sea level).

At the end of the first lap Stanley was in front, followed by Jimmy Simpson (AJS) and Frank Longman (Rudge). Lap two, Simpson led Stanley, and by the third lap, with rain lashing down, Stanley led Simpson, from

his clutch checked, but he never told this to Woods. Had he had better knowledge of his huge lead, he could have eased the pace and things might have worked out differently.

After his disappointment in the TT, he had the rich consolation on the continent of winning three major

The Winner

The Unapproachable Norton

The DUTCH INTERNATIONAL T.T.

FOR the first time in the history of the race, the Dutch T.T. became an International race in 1927. In order, however, that national entries should still feel that it was their own particular race, a separate category for National riders was provided.

The race was held on the Drenthe Circuit near Assen on June 25th, 1927, over 16 laps, each of approximately 10¾ miles, and lay over a difficult and narrow course.

The Senior International Event was won by Stanley Woods on a Norton, at an average of 67.02 m.p.h.—a record speed, and five minutes in front of second man home.

The National event was won by Mr. A. P. van Hamersveld, also riding a 490 c.c. Norton. It is interesting to recall that the Dutch T.T. races of 1925 and 1926 were each won by Mr. P. van Wyngaarden on Nortons —so that Norton machines have won the event three years in succession.

Stanley Woods, fresh and happy after winning the Dutch International T.T. and, in oval, Mr. A. P. van Hamersveld, winner of the National event

The Unapproachable

Norton

The
SWISS GRAND PRIX

THE Swiss Grand Prix of 1927 was the first in which an Official Norton rider had entered. The Senior Race for machines up to 500 c.c. was held on July 10th, over the Circuit de Meyrin, near Geneva—a course of the usual continental triangular type, and the distance was 248 miles.

This was another splendid victory for that wonderfully successful Norton rider, Stanley Woods. Beside putting up a record lap at 75.4 m.p.h.—a fine performance—Woods won the event at a record speed of 70.5 m.p.h. Once again the Norton proved its wonderful capacity on pastures new—and the favourable comments that followed this magnificent "first appearance victory," was very gratifying to Norton enthusiasts in Switzerland.

Above: Stanley Woods on his wonderful O.H. Camshaft Norton, and below, on one of the numerous bends approaching Geneva.

Belgian Grand Prix.	1st
Norton	150 . 0 . 0
K.L.G.	30 . 0 . 0
Renold .	15 . 0 . 0
Castrol	50 . 0 . 0
Terry	20 . 0 . 0
Binks	10 . 0 . 0
Dunlop	100 . 0 . 0
£	375 . 0 . 0

Henne and Walker (Sunbeam). Lap four, Simpson was out with gearbox trouble, and Stanley fell at speed on wet concrete on a left bend, just below the start. This was the first time he had experienced rain and concrete in a race. Walker then led the field and although he had lost five minutes after the tumble, by the finish Stanley had worked his way through to second place 57 seconds in arrears of the winner Graham Walker.

1927 UGP

Huge crowds gathered for Ireland's premier road race. Some had camped overnight, others cycled, most walked from the end of the Tram Terminus at Ligoneil, North Belfast. The 500 race, one of the closest of the pre-war races, had Jimmy Shaw, Joe Craig and Stanley Woods entered on the new 'Camshaft Norton.' For four laps Craig and Woods entertained the large Ulster crowd, fighting it out wheel to wheel, but on the fifth lap Craig's oil tank ran dry and his engine seized. All this had taken the edge off Stanley's engine, and he was eventually caught and passed by both Shaw and Frank Longman (Rudge). Stanley finished third, 10 seconds behind Longman, but with the consolation of setting a new course record at 78.26 mph.

Ulster Grand Prix

1928

With Stanley now a full-time professional racer, things were not so good for Ted Woods, Stanley's father; who had seen a steady decline in business and by now had resigned from Mackintosh's. Further, there had been a fire at their family home and amongst the personal items lost were all of Stanley's early correspondence from

Cotton, Norton etc. However, in late 1927, he hit on the idea of using most of the money that he had earned up to then for the flotation of a new company, with his father, to manufacture toffee – 'TT Toffees' - Where did the name come from?

A well known firm in Dublin at that time was B. B. Toffees and Stanley, by then a double 'Island winner,' decided that the TT brand name would give optimum opportunity for publicity. On the 4th April 1928 the new company was announced. Toffee was mainly sold to children and normally there were five pieces to the ounce, but Stanley pulled a clever one by having his trays made so as to render 'six pieces to the ounce'. As well as seeming to give more for the money, it actually made better sense, because you cannot divide five lumps of toffee between two or three children.

Those last years of the decade were dismal times as far as racing and the Norton team were concerned.

Walter Moore had redesigned the cylinder head and as a result the engines were prone to overheating and were also down on power from the previous year's machines. Norton Motors took part in the Junior Class of the TT for the first time, with Jimmy Guthrie a full team member, following his runner-up spot in the previous year on the New Hudson. Alec Bennett won on a Velocette, having arranged to ride it before Norton had a 350. It was not a successful debut, as all of Norton's five Junior entries retired.

In the Senior, Stanley was the only team member to finish, a lowly fifth behind a Sunbeam, A.J.S., Scott and Rudge, while Frank Longman won the Lightweight on an OK Supreme. He led throughout the race and won by seventeen minutes.

Stanley won the 350 class of the Dutch TT but retired in the 500 class while in the French GP at Bordeaux he scored the only Norton 500 class win of the year.

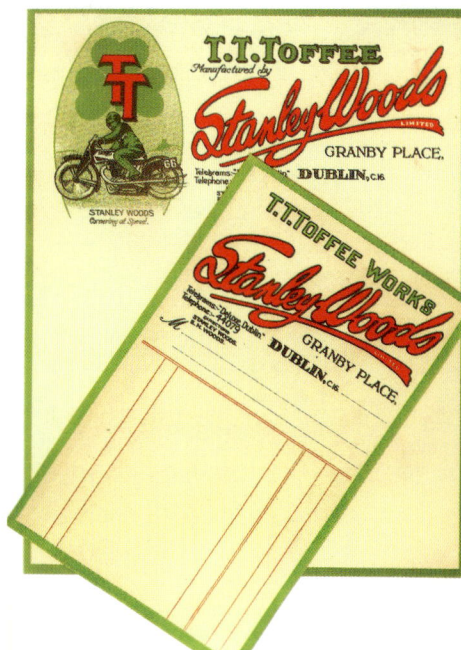

In the German GP, Nortons entered four machines, the races being run concurrently. There were two 500s for Stanley and Joe Craig (both retired) and 350s for Jimmy Guthrie and Pietro Ghersi, who won ahead of Guthrie after a very long race.

Things were no better at the Belgian GP, with both the 500s and 350s being non-finishers.

The Norton riders never brought mechanics with them and after a race Joe Craig, Jimmy Guthrie and Stanley would usually take four machines into the official marquee, remove the petrol tanks and cylinder heads for measuring, check the valves and reassemble them fit for practice at the next event. The other two team members took no part in this activity.

Courtesy National Museums Northern Ireland

Stanley, Winner 350cc Class, Dutch TT

The Unapproachable Norton

The French Grand Prix

SURELY the organisers of the French Grand Prix must have set out to create some really exciting sport when they chose the difficult course at Bordeaux as the venue of the 1928 race, held on June 30th. There were some glorious "straights" admittedly, but there were also some of the trickiest roads that even France could produce. To put it quite mildly, this was a "difficult" circuit, as many riders quickly discovered. But with Stanley Woods in the saddle of a Norton, difficulties are turned into opportunities. With excellent judgment and complete faith in the ability of his Norton, this hard riding speedman made the very most of every yard of straight and thrilled the onlookers with his fine cornering and smart manoeuvring. Once again this Race was a "Norton" outing, for Woods won the race of 204 miles at an average speed of 67.62 m.p.h. and incidentally made a record lap at 71.64. The following table shows Norton history in French Grand Prix races. Need more be said.

1924	First	Alec Bennett	490 c.c. Norton.
1925	Second	Joe Craig	490 c.c. Norton.
1926	First	Alec Bennett	490 c.c. Norton.
1927	First	Joe Craig	490 c.c. Norton.
1928	First	Stanley Woods	490 c.c. Norton.

Stanley Woods receiving the Trophy and being congratulated in the best French manner, after winning.

The winner making final preparations for the start of the French Grand Prix.

500 c.c. French Grand Prix. 1st

Dunlop Tyres	50 . 0 . 0
Renold Chains	25 . 0 . 0
Terry Saddles	20 . 0 . 0
K.L.G. Plugs	30 . 0 . 0
Prize Money 1st	35 . 19 . 5
Castrol Oil	50 . 0 . 0
Norton	100 . 0 . 0
£	310 . 19 . 5

STANLEY'S WORDS - SWISS GP

"During 1928/29 I was flogging a 'Dead Horse' and taking risks that were bound to lead to trouble. In '28 when the 500 Nortons were eclipsed, Joe Craig and I were scrapping with Walter Handley (on a 500 Motosacoche) in the Swiss GP and on wet tar (melting in the sun), Joe locked his front wheel and crashed, bringing me down as well, he damaged his knee and did not race again. I damaged my back and although shaken, remounted only to run out of road at a hairpin a few miles further on, due to the brakes having been damaged.

Incidentally I forgot that the previous day in the 350 race, a sudden thunder storm had soaked the road at the pits on the lap that I was due to refill. The pits where situated on the straight just over the brow of a hill and I did not know that the road was wet and slippery, the bike slid out from under me and on down the centre of the road almost exactly to my pit. I slid after it more or less sitting at ease on the wet polished surface, much to the amusement of the grandstand. No damage to bike or self but the buttons came off the back of my pants. Thereafter until I retired with a broken petrol pipe; I rode with the tail of my shirt flying in the wind. The promoters presented me with a special prize, whether for 'pluck and endurance' or 'light relief' I shall never know."

Walter Handley did the double for Motosacoche winning the 350 and 500 classes of the Swiss GP and the Grand Prix of Europe. (The title 'Grand Prix of Europe' a name awarded to just one classic each year, making it in name at least the most important Grand Prix of the season).

The trouble continued at the Ulster GP for Stanley, Alec Bennett and Jimmy Simpson, who was riding for Norton for the first time, with Shaw and Guthrie on the new 350s.

Shaw was the only finisher of the team in third place behind Frank Longman (Velocette) and Leo Davenport (AJS); Longman's winning speed was even faster than the 1927 Senior TT which was also a record. Alec Bennett was arguably the greatest rider of the decade, a quiet unassuming Ulsterman who had migrated to Canada at an early age. After service with the RFC in World War 1, he returned to the UK. Successes with Sunbeams early in the decade led on to 1924, when he was the first rider to win three major classics, the French (known then only as the "Grand Prix"), the Belgian and the Senior TT, all on Norton machines. He was also the first rider to demonstrate that a TT could be won with 'Brain rather than Brawn' and was the one rider on whom Stanley modelled himself.

Norton Team, Ulster Grand Prix

Incidentally, it was in this year that Stanley used cord breeches and then later, a complete green corduroy suit!

OCTOBER/NOVEMBER 1928

Back in Dublin on 13th October, at Harold's Cross Speedway dirt track, riding a 500 Douglas he quickly mastered the unfamiliar art of 'Broadsiding' to set up new 'Course' and 'Standing start' records, winning two of the handicapped heats and finishing second in another from scratch.

In November he won the Dublin University MCC Bush Cup Trial and the Boxing Day Trial both on a Norton CS1 loaned to him by the company.

1929

The year started well, with a win in the Patland Cup (hailed as the trial of trials), on a 490 cc Norton. In the Athy 75, he came through to win the 500 class from the

Harolds Cross Speedway

scratch mark by half a minute, with fastest lap plus a third in the Senior class of the inaugural North West 200.

Joe Craig thought that he knew where the problems lay with Norton's race engines, but Bill Mansell (Norton's MD) had decided to give Walter Moore another chance to rectify things. Craig had by then given up racing and acquired a motor garage where he had previously been employed in Ballymena; he left Birmingham and moved back to N. Ireland.

The team for the TT was Stanley, Hunt, Guthrie, Simpson and for the first time the machines had Sturmey-Archer positive-stop foot-change gearboxes.

ATHY SEVENTY-FIVE
again won on
WAKEFIELD
CASTROL
MOTOR OIL

Reproduced by courtesy of "The Motor Cycle"
Mr. Stanley Woods' winning smile!

1st Stanley Woods
490 NORTON
Speed 69.6 m p.h.

3rd G. E. Nott
499 RUDGE

—also the 4th, 5th, 6th, 7th, 8th, 10th and 11th all used *Wakefield* CASTROL!

In 1928 also this race was won on CASTROL, which was used by every finisher except one!

So CASTROL continues its winning way! And remember that *every* I.O.M. Tourist Trophy Race for the past five years has been won on Wakefield CASTROL—and the Senior for 13 times in succession. These facts are significant—for the utmost speed with reliability you *must* use CASTROL.

C. C. WAKEFIELD & CO., LTD.
All British Firm,
Wakefield House, London, E.C.2.

FOUR MORE WORLD'S RECORDS AT BROOKLANDS

On May 15th, Mr. M. V. McCudden, riding Mr. J. S. Worter's

250 EXCELSIOR - J.A.P.

broke the following World's Records in Class A, subject to confirmation.

100 Miles - 74.30 m.p.h.
200 Miles - 73.25 m.p.h.
2 Hours - 73.01 m.p.h.
3 Hours - 73.25 m.p.h.

—of course, using CASTROL

Charlie Manders and Tom Byrne, Portmarnock

Hunt, incidentally, had been invited to join the team after winning the 1927 and 1928 Senior Amateur TT events – mounted on Nortons. During practice for the Junior, Jimmy Guthrie crashed and was a non-starter. Freddie Hicks won another Junior for Velocette while all the 350 Nortons retired.

The Senior started on wet roads and throughout lap one Stanley's best was a lowly fifth place. On lap two, Hunt moved up to fourth place, on his third lap he broke the lap record at 73.12 mph and this put him in

1927 Norton 490cc CS1, Reg. KS3900. Stanley won countless off-road events on this machine

Norton Team with Tom Byrne (second from right)

the lead by three seconds. The race was so close at that stage that Stanley was still in fifth place and only 35 seconds behind the race leader Charlie Dodson (Sunbeam). Hunt crashed at Quarterbridge on his fourth lap and wiped off a footrest, picked himself up, continued, crashed again at Waterworks, lost the other footrest and restarted again. He finally finished fourth. On lap five Stanley's race came to an end when he crashed heavily, hitting the bank, just going into Kirkmichael.

50 years later, during TT week in 1979, Stanley and I were invited to watch the Senior from the garden of Stanley and Jessie Keig, who had a nice bungalow across from the Mitre Inn in the village. During the race Mrs. Keig brought us out a tray with tea and cakes: she remembered Stanley coming off at the top of the village when she was about eleven years old.

Stanley told us then that his pit just kept signalling to go faster, but gave him no information as to his race position. He recalled getting a substantial injury to his mouth and chin in his spill, some of his front teeth coming loose as a result. One dentist advised him that he would have to have teeth removed, but he sought the

opinion of a second dentist who advised him to use wooden tooth picks, with regular use and massaging the gums, things eventually got back to normal and he never wore dentures, even into his 90th year.

Stanley was wearing a Services shock-proof watch, as worn by noted TT riders, it cost fifteen shillings and sixpence and after the crash it was in perfect working order.

The TT of 1929 was a turning point for Stanley and his discontent with the Norton team because of their poor results. He was also beginning to lose confidence in himself, at twenty-six years of age; he thought that his career as a racing motorcyclist was over and was considering retirement.

One evening whilst walking along the Glencrutchery road inspecting the road surfaces etc., as he often did, he was carrying a large magnet on a string, for most of the traffic was horse drawn, discharging horseshoe nails all over the course. Indeed, punctures at the most awkward moments were one of the most common causes of race retirements. It never ceased to amaze him just how many nails he could collect in an evening.

Stanley (Norton) at Ramsey

During his stroll he spotted a two storey house just past the pits with a telephone line running to it and the upstairs bedroom window within sight of the start. This offered the opportunity he had been looking for, to improve the information that he received from signals during a race. His aim, if he could obtain the owner's permission, was to connect this telephone with another across the course. However, he decided that this plan would have to wait until he had a competitive machine. In the Lightweight TT, Pietro Ghersi led until the end of the fifth lap, broke down in the sixth and Sid Crabtree won on an Excelsior.

In the RAC Ulster Tourist Trophy car race, Stanley Woods and passenger Gordon Burney from Dublin entered in a Lea Francis. Both were well known as racing motorcyclists, so had their performance watched closely by Irish spectators. They did not have long to watch, for both were soon added to the increasing roll of retirements, with a bent front axle

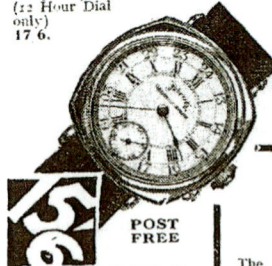

Scenes before Ulster TT with Ernie Mitchell, Stanley and Lea Francis car

Joe Craig – The Professor

after an accident. All of the eight Lea Francis cars entered failed to finish.

Norton chief designer Walter Moore had left and gone to Germany to take up a job with NSU and Bill Mansell had invited Joe Craig back to Birmingham to take over the preparation of the works racers and the development of all production racing machines. Craig, also known as the 'Professor,' had a deep understanding of engines and an impressive record as a rider. He was a debut winner in the 600 class of Ulster Grand Prix in 1923 on a borrowed Norton, his first ever race, and before that he had never taken part in competition of any kind.

The 1929 Ulster Grand Prix, run in a heat wave, was won by Graham Walker on a 500cc Rudge Whitworth at a record speed of 80.63mph plus a fastest lap of 82.36mph. This time, thanks to Craig and Carroll having resolved the overheating problem, the Nortons finished, with Tim Hunt taking second place and Stanley third.

STANLEY'S WORDS Carrowdore 100 18th September

"I persuaded Nortons to let me have a machine for a race at Carrowdore, Co. Down, 'I rode her to earth' in a spectacular rear wheel slide with slight damage to dignity and back, with considerable damage to machine. After that

KS 3900 nearly up to the carburetor in water on a Trial

Nortons clamped down and said, "No Larking about in local races!" and quite right too, for the handicappers made it quite impossible for me to win.

The danger element on these 'back road circuits' was far too great with possibly a full season of International Races at stake! So that was the last local event I rode in."

He did continue to ride Nortons in the Leinster and North West 200 races, in the Phoenix Park 10 mile Championship on September 28th he came first and won six trials in that season.

Stanley and Hunt went down to Barcelona for the Spanish Grand Prix, where Hunt won and Stanley retired with big-end trouble.

Stanley then finished the year as he had started by winning an important trial, The Dublin University Motorcycle Club Bush Cup on 7th December. Nevertheless, Nortons' 1930 sales catalogue, 'The Roadholder', would have very little to proclaim by way of success during the 1929 season.

Senior TT

1930
PHOENIX PARK CHAMPIONSHIPS

At the championship meeting held in the Phoenix Park on August 16th, Stanley Woods was the hero of the meeting, winning both 500cc 10 Mile Solo and 25 mile sidecar titles and making fastest time from scratch, notwithstanding the fact that he was riding a Norton that was nearly 3 years old, that had been ridden in

Trials, Grass-track and Sand racing events.

(It is worthy of note that the Phoenix Park is the largest enclosed park in Europe).

He then raced at the Athy club's Grass-track meeting at the Curragh the following day, winning two events, the 600cc race and the Open Handicap.

On August 30th at the Knock Motorcycle Club grass-track meeting on the Maze Race Course near Lisburn, one of the spectators remarked, *"It would be worth*

Stanley's 490 CS1 Norton, Phoenix Park

Grasstrack

On the sand with Jim Cummings in the sidecar

Violet Woods with Gordon's outfit

coming miles to see Stanley Woods going round that bend if there was nobody else in the race".

In this 20 mile handicap race Stanley won, outclassing the rest of the riders for sheer speed and rode in a breathtaking fashion, despite conceding a time allowance of eleven minutes and ten seconds to the limit man.

Stanley in the mud

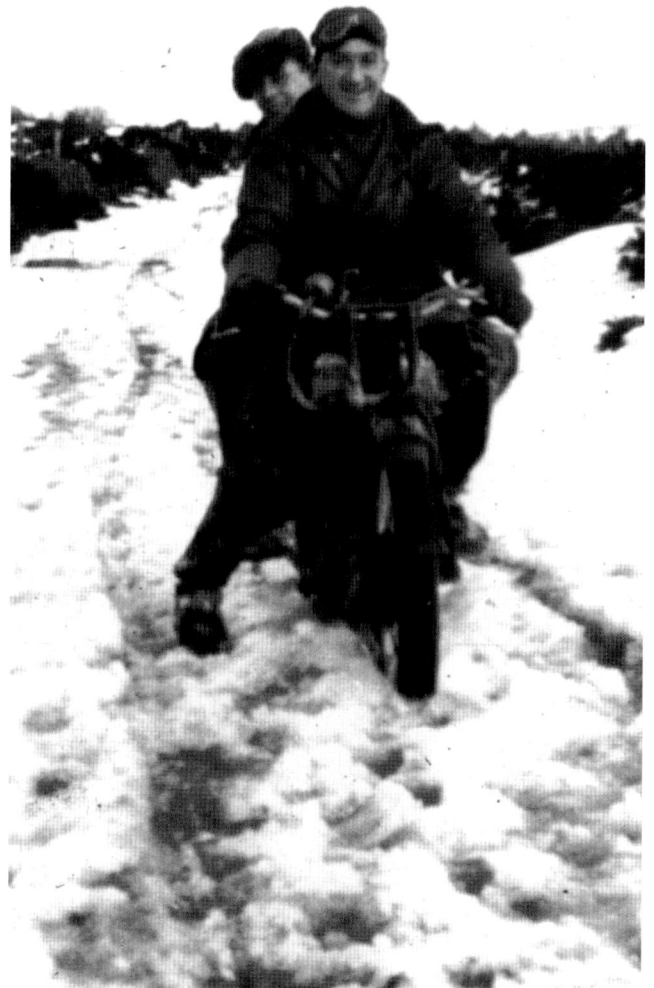

St Patrick's Day Trial

UGP SEPTEMBER 6th 500 CLASS

Since the 1928, season the Norton team had suffered a bad run of failures, the first camshaft engines were unreliable. Woods once remarked that *"You would be lucky to finish a race with a complete set of bevels"*.

The firms' 'Technical Wizards' Joe Craig and Arthur Carrol joined forces to develop a new camshaft engine that contained the basis of a design that would rocket Norton to world fame.

In the TT that year, the best that Stanley could manage was 6th in the Junior and he retired in the Senior. After another disappointing TT, Stanley finished 2nd behind Graham Walker in both 500cc classes of the German GP and the Dutch TT.

The machines were too new, heavy, and not particularly quick, but back at the factory they managed to get the weight down considerably.

Jimmy Simpson took one of these machines to Saxtorp and won the 500 class of Swedish GP with instructions to phone Bracebridge Street to inform them of his results.

This was the signal for Joe Craig to go ahead with the bikes for the Ulster, now with two stay frames. Simpson became the 'Worlds Fastest Road Racer' at the Ulster Grand Prix, when it was announced that J. H. Simpson, 'Norton' had lapped the course at the terrific average speed of 84.64 miles per hour, before he blew up yet again.

Graham Walker, winner of the previous two years and holder of the lap record, who was hoping for a hat-trick, went out of the race after covering two laps, then it became a 'red hot fight' between Stanley Woods (Norton), Charlie Dodson (Sunbeam) and Henry Tyrell Smith (Rudge). Stanley set the pace and Dodson tore after him, sometimes only two seconds separated the pair, with Tyrell Smith hard on their heels. Whatever Dodson did, Woods went one better and managed to shake off one of the keenest challenges ever seen in a race, winning by 13 seconds.

Interviewed after the race, Stanley said, *"I was always aware of the danger from Dodson and was travelling at ¾ or throttle until the last two laps when flat out, I knew that*

Stanley's first UGP win for Norton

A businesslike-looking weapon with which to fight the T.T. battle—but the 1930 Norton didn't win the T.T. Nonetheless, it was developed to sweep the board in 1931, and for a long time afterwards, with very few engine modifications.

1930 **NORTON 500**

I won the 1930 Ulster Grand Prix on this one & also the 1931 1932 & 1933 U.G.P. on its successors.

Stanley Woods

1930 500cc Norton

Prize money for the 500 Winner

500 cc.	Ulster Grand Prix.	1st
Prize Money.	£15 – 0 – 0
M².ₐ Magnetos	25 . 0 . 0
Renold Chains	25 . 0 . 0
Amal Carbs.	7 . 10 . 0
Wellworthy rings	10 . 0 . 0
Dunlop Tyres	50 . 0 . 0
Dunlop Saddles	10 . 0 . 0
Lodge Plugs	30 . 0 . 0
Ferodo Brakes	30 . 0 . 0
Pratts Petrol	10 . 0 . 0
Castrol Oil	50 . 0 . 0
Norton Motors	100 . 0 . 0
	£ 362 . 10 . 0

Dodson was hard after me, but I also knew that barring accidents I could just beat him, at times on the straights I was touching 107 miles per hour, passing the Grandstands I think I was doing 100 mph each time". The race distance was 12 laps of 21 miles a total of 252 miles.

The year had started with a 2nd in the Patland Cup Trial, a 3rd place from scratch in the NW200 and ended with an easy win in the 500 class of the French GP at Pau. Gaining premier awards in the Curragh Grass-track, two wins in the Dublin University Motorcycle Club events, the Fall Trial and the Bush Cup Trial again, all Norton mounted.

It was during the glorious decade of the 1930s that Stanley would become the best known Irishman in the world.

NEW ENGINES

On the home front, Stanley again put his name on the 'Patland Cup' for the fourth time, the St. Patrick's Day Trial and the Leinster MCC Easter Trial on the old 'Moore Norton'. The new engines had their first outing at Ireland's North West 200, where in the Senior race it was expected that Stanley would end the Rudge run of success. Ernie Nott led for the first five laps, then Stanley took the lead, broke the lap record (75.36 mph), but four laps later he developed a soft rear tyre. Nott regained the lead and Stanley finished second, 4 minutes in arrears. A week later in the Leinster 200, Stanley rode Tim Hunt's 350 in the 'Big Race' and was leading until forced to retire with a puncture.

In early 1931, while in London, he spotted and bought a 1927 Delage International Sport, with Weyman fabric body. It gave years of reliable service including many trips to Europe, until he finally sold it to an enthusiast in Dublin in 1949.

Stanley once told that it was not until 1931 TT practice that they realised just how good the new engines were, if so he might have brought forward by a year the use of the private 'Signalling System' that he had in mind, as Norton's were well-nigh unbeatable.

Despite this, the best that he could manage was fourth place in the Junior and third in the Senior. He

the start, and after a few laps, the veteran Belgian rider Renier on a privately owned Velocette put Woods into third spot. To make things worse, Woods knew that Renier had a son, his own age in the same race. A fierce scrap developed for second place and the matter was decided when Renier over did it on a slow corner with loose surface.

After the race, Stanley's machine was sent back to Birmingham and he learnt later that his rear mudguard had been distorted and had been bearing on the tyre, so losing him quite a bit of speed. Seven days later, not in a very confident mood, he would ride in the German Grand Prix.

rode for most of the 350cc race with a broken steering damper, while in the Senior race he had to put up with a slight spray of petrol to his face and goggles from a faulty fuel-cap. After refuelling he attempted to restart with the ignition too far advanced and twice failed to get away, so losing precious time.

Although, in his opinion these were only minor troubles, he was not satisfied with his performances and was again considering retirement.

Tim Hunt made history by winning both Junior and Senior Trophies and with Jimmy Guthrie second and Stanley third, Norton registered the first ever Senior hat-trick by a British manufacturer.

At the French GP, a road race at Montlhery on June 29th, Ernie Nott (350 Rudge) took the lead right from

STANLEY'S WORDS

"It was obvious then that the team was unbeatable and on the Continent it was 'Orders'. That season it was, put up a show until the last lap and then fight it out!

The two Jimmies were on the 350's and Tim Hunt and I on the 500's. In that race at the Nurburgring I beat Tim by ½ a wheel, after the most hectic ride of my career, he was actually over-taking me on the line. On dismantling his engine the piston was found to be cracked, obviously from over-revving. This re-established my own self-confidence which was down a little after the Isle of Man. Fortunately for both of us we did not clash again in a last

Stanley, winner of the Dutch TT 350 Class, chasing Sid Gleave

lap duel as Tim had always some minor delay, otherwise one or both of us would have crashed. We and Joe Craig realised this, so in the autumn, discussions produced the final orders for 1932. In the TT, 3rd lap positions to be maintained, in the Grand Prix, each would win in turn and prize money (if any) plus bonus shared

After the German Grand Prix Stanley with renewed confidence he said *"If I could beat Tim Hunt at the Nurburgring then I can beat anybody anywhere"*

One week later Norton scored a 'Double Dutch' at the Van Drente circuit, Assen in the North of Holland, with Hunt winning the 500cc Class achieving a world record lap of 84.99mph ahead of Ernie Nott (Rudge). Having to cope with a broken clutch lever Stanley came third down by just 8 seconds and also won the 350cc race.

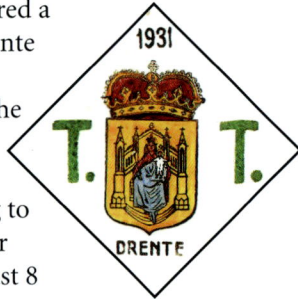

A short journey took them to Spa for the Belgium GP on 19th July where he won the 250 mile race in wet and miserable conditions; Hunt retired with a puncture, the 350 Class run concurrently and was won by Guthrie.

With nearly a month before the next classic the team had time off while the machines were prepared in Birmingham, for the Swiss GP in Berne on 15/16th August. The 350 Class, held on the Saturday, was won by Hunt with Stanley runner up. On Sunday Stanley won the 500 Class with two records - average speed of

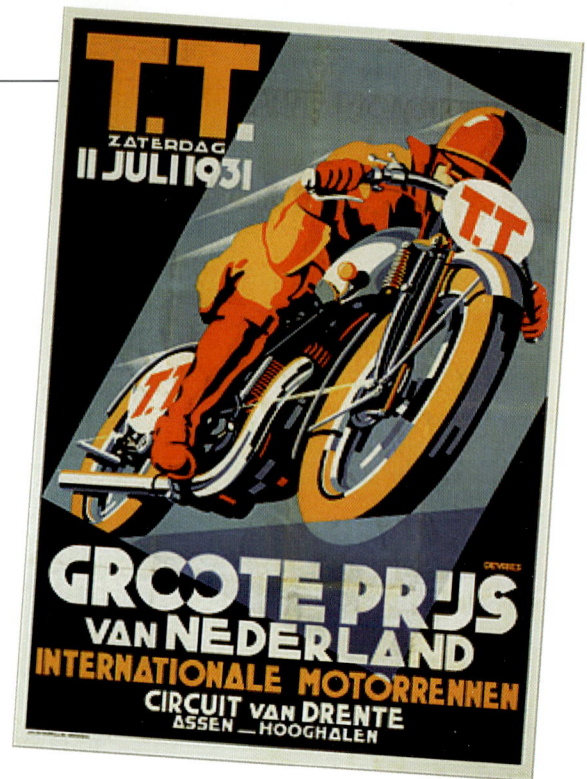

73.41mph & lap of 77.74. Hunt retired with engine trouble.

The Ulster Grand Prix on 15th September saw Stanley teamed with Simpson and Hunt for the 500 race. Ernie Nott (Rudge), Arthur Simcock (OK Supreme) and Stanley (Norton) set the pace from the start and by the

Start, Belgium GP

Pit stop, Belgium GP

Stanley and Jimmy, 500cc & 350cc Class winners

Joe Craig (far left) with winner

Winner 500cc, Swiss GP

end of lap two, the leader, Nott, was averaging 85.30 mph. All went well for a while until Clady Corner at the end of the third lap, Stanley's clutch control fractured, just as it did at Assen, eight weeks before.

He realised that with another nine laps to go it was likely that some part of the transmission would give

trouble owing to the terrific strain that would be imposed by changing gear without de-clutching. With this in mind he decided to attempt one really fast lap and then retire if necessary.

Riding, as he had never ridden before, he put in a 4th lap of 13 minutes 43 seconds - 89.67mph – a record, which regained the title of 'The Worlds Fastest Road Race' for the 'Ulster' that lap record stood for three years.

Establishing such a lead he was able to ride comparatively easy and nurse his machine for the rest of the race and win by a comfortable margin from Nott with Hunt 3rd.

This really was an astonishing performance, what a tribute to a superb rider and to ride for most of the race with the clutch lever missing.

A young unknown 21 year old rider, Walter F. Rusk, entered his first Ulster Grand Prix. W J Chambers had been impressed with Walter's riding in local races and offered him a ride on a 500 AJS, which had previously been ridden by Freddie Hicks. On one lap it was announced that he managed to raise the lap record to 87.54 mph, only bettered by Stanley, the eventual

Shaw's garage Belfast LtoR Jimmy Shaw, Harry Palmer, Stanley Woods, Wesley Shaw, Jimmy Simpson, Jimmy Guthrie and mechanic Bill Mewis

At Aldergrove, clutch lever missing

Stanley with Ton Byrne at Portmarnock

STANLEY'S WORDS

"In 1932, I think this is why I didn't put more money into the Toffee factory.

I bought a house, it was really a mansion on the outskirts of Dublin with six & a half acres of grounds for £2,500, it had its own river with its own hydro-electric scheme running through the grounds, there were four green houses. I employed a gardener at 30 shillings per week, 5 ½ days – good money in those days and he was 'as happy as Larry'.

I'll tell you how big the house was – we moved into it in the spring of 1932, that year Norton did not want to come to the Leinster 200 for some reason or another. I suggested that I would put the team up for the three or four days, Joe Craig, Jimmy Guthrie, Jimmy Simpson & Arthur Bourne of the 'Motorcycle' were my guests and we had a right good time. I think that there are 300 houses on that ground now in Dundrum South Co Dublin".

winner. Unfortunately the inlet valve spring broke on the penultimate lap when he was in fourth place, behind Stanley, Nott and Hunt.

AJS had pulled out of racing following Freddie Hicks' death in the TT, but the directors sent Rusk a telegram congratulating him on his performance and apologizing for the fact that this particular bike handled very badly. Stanley, on the old Norton, won the Dublin University Motorcycle Club Fall Trial and also rode in The Scott Trial, the 5 mile Championship and two other grass tracks, gaining mostly first places.

1932

Now in his thirtieth year, it opened with another victory in the Patland Cup on the time tested 1927 Norton. This remarkable machine, though not a pukka race model, enabled him to win countless victories in all kinds of off-road events over a five year period. It was the Olympia Show bike, described by him many years later as "a real friend" and after he left Norton in the fall of 1933, it was returned to Birmingham.

The post 1929 global depression was beginning to bite, motorcycle manufacturers were cutting back on their expenditure due to poor sales, accessory firms were supporting fewer competitors, and to make matters worse he had been putting more of his earnings into his ailing Toffee Factory in Dublin, which had been hit hard. By April 1932 he could see no future in toffee, closed it down and paid all his creditors "twenty shillings to the pound".

That same spring, Stanley entered the 'Trade' in partnership with Charlie Manders (a well known young

Cheerful Charlie Manders

Dublin rider) to sell Sunbeam, New Hudson, Levis and Newmount motorcycles. Manders entered a Rudge engined Newmount in the 1931 Junior TT, the marque's only appearance in the TT. Manders was always well placed in the Lightweight TT on privately entered Rudge, New Imperial and Excelsior between 1933-1938 but this motorcycle agency closed after eighteen months.

The road racing season of 1932 began as usual with Ireland's North West 200 and Leinster 200 events in May, regarded by the big racing firms as warm ups for the TT. Stanley had a stroke of bad luck, when on the first lap of the NW200 a sheared spark plug cost him a time of 19 mins 35 secs, for the first circuit. Stanley never had a harder ride and clawed back his time deficiency to 9 mins 6 secs and finished third, with a retirement in the Leinster with an empty oil tank.

In the years since his clutch failure in the 1927 Senior TT, Stanley had thought very carefully about a workable signalling system and now decided to introduce it, for he felt he had a machine he could win on as Nortons had proved themselves to be absolutely unapproachable, using larger petrol tanks which ensured a 'single stop' in a seven lap TT and switching from lever to 'twist grip throttle' as the personal choice of each rider.

His private signalling system was now put into place - The house on the Glencrutchery Rd just past the pits on the right hand side and within sight of the start, was interconnected by telephone to a point selected across the course which was the public telephone box at Sulby crossroads. This arrangement would enable him to receive two signals per lap, instead of just the customary one as he passed the pits. He arranged with the operators at the telephone exchange for an account to be set up, making it possible to pay afterwards and bribed the operators with boxes of chocolates in order to give his calls priority - all such activities being carried out in great secrecy.

This was before the advent of direct-dialling and all calls had to go through the operator, so about ten minutes before the start, his brother-in-law Gordon Burney (himself a TT rider), the legendary Irish timekeeper, originally born in the Isle of Man, Athole Harrison with the help of other trusted local enthusiasts would lift the receiver at the Sulby phone box (known as No 1 Station) ask to be put through to the house on the Glencrutchery Road (known as No 2 Station), the line was then left open throughout the race.

Athole Harrison, timekeeper

Actual Sulby Timepiece, 1932-1939

No I Signalling Station, Sulby Crossroads

With team orders now in place, it was understood that whichever member of the team was leading at the end of the third lap would be left with the lead. For Stanley this meant he would have to ride harder in the early stages to gain the lead, which was the opposite of his usual plan, which was to take it easy and wait for the faster men to fall out. It would now be a three lap free for all.

JUNIOR TT

The 1932 Junior TT, produced a shock result, for only one of six Nortons finished. Fortunately, Stanley was riding the one which did finish and he led throughout, in a great race which turned into a Norton/Rudge duel. Hunt and Simpson retired with engine trouble and Guthrie crashed. Handley brought his Rudge into second place, with Tyrell Smith on another Rudge third.

SENIOR TT

1932 was the year of the first Royal TT, with the Senior attended by HRH Prince George, Duke of Kent. Jimmy Simpson set the pace as usual with a

Walter Handley, runner-up, congratulating Junior Winner

Crowds cheer Stanley on last lap of Junior TT

H.R.H. Prince George Duke of Kent shakes hands with Stanley before the start of the 1932 Senior TT. Norton directors Gilbert Smith & Dennis Mansell look on

record lap of 81.50 mph, with Stanley 2nd and Walter
Handley (Rudge) 3rd. On the next lap, Handley crashed
at Barregarrow, Stanley took the lead and stayed there to
the end, winning from Jimmy Guthrie by over two
minutes, with Jimmy Simpson 3rd. Norton scored their
second 1-2-3 Senior in succession and Stanley became
only the second man in TT history to do a Junior/Senior
double.

That year Stanley elected to change to a bright
orange helmet so that he could easily and instantly be
recognised by his signalling staff. He purchased a new
two piece horse-hide racing suit and a pair of cavalry
style boots from Lewis of Great Portland St, London and
wore chamois gloves instead of the gauntlets as worn by
other riders. Stanley was meticulous about his personal
preparation, everything buckled, tied or laced properly
with nothing left to chance.

The Dutch TT held on the 25th June, resulted in a first
in the 350 class for Stanley with Hunt 2nd, with the
order reversed for the 500 class. Then it was Stanley first and
Hunt 2nd in the 350 class of the French GP at Rheims.

At the Belgian GP held on the 17th July, yet another
500 victory for Stanley after Hunt fell and broke his
collar bone on the left hand bend below the pits, as he
tried to adjust his goggles.

The Swiss GP held on July 30-31st, Stanley had easy
wins in both classes.

Stanley and Tim Hunt, Dutch TT

*Signpost
Corner*

Villa Marina LtoR Dennis Mansell, Stanley holding the Senior Tourist Trophy, Prince George presenting the Manx Government Certificate

Lieutenant Governor

ISLE OF MAN
INTERNATIONAL AUTO-CYCLE TOURIST TROPHY RACES
1932

This is to Certify

that the FIRST PRIZE awarded
by THE MANX GOVERNMENT for
THE AUTO-CYCLE UNION SENIOR
TOURIST TROPHY RACE
run in the Isle of Man on the 10th June 1932
was won by

STANLEY WOODS

riding a NORTON Motor Cycle,
the average speed being 79·38 miles per hour.

Government Secretary

Piccadilly Cigarette Cards

Coming off flying boat at Dun Laoghaire harbour

UGP Stanley's sister Violet with husband Gordon Burney (OK Supreme)

UGP

The 11th Ulster Grand Prix was held on 3rd September, a disappointing year for spectators as the weather was atrocious. In the Senior race Woods took the lead almost from the start. At the end of the sixth lap he re-fuelled and after that he was never really challenged. There were only three finishers, Stanley, Hunt (Norton) with Arthur Simcock (Rudge) third; Stanley had won his third consecutive Senior UGP with a fastest lap of 87.65 mph.

For him it was another fantastic year, even though in the above events he had to share his prize money with team mate Tim Hunt to meet team orders, with the exception of the Swiss double victory where Hunt had been a non-starter after his Belgian accident.

1933

Stanley never had much luck in the North West 200, where 1933 saw, for the first time, the closing of the roads for official practice. He took the lead from the start and won the Senior class by a huge margin, with fastest lap, 77.71 mph. Prize money was a modest £9, plus £5 bonus from Dunlop.

His retainer from Norton had reduced from £350 in other years to £250 in 1933 and there were no bonuses that season. Previously they paid their riders £50 to £100 for wins in major races.

Prize money from the ACU and Grand Prix organizers had also suffered, plus companies such as Dunlop Tyres, Lodge Spark Plugs & Renold Chains had cut back considerably on their bonus payments to successful riders using their products, while others disappeared from the scene.

This was the year in which Stanley married Marie Louise Henriette Dumontel from Lyon, whom he had met during his many trips to France. They set up home in Dublin, but sadly it did not work out and they parted after only a few months.

At the June races on the Isle of Man, Norton who had dominated the class since 1931 swept the board in the Junior & Senior for the second year. Stanley, leading the combination of Simpson, Guthrie and Hunt broke the lap record in both classes, and became the first man in TT history to do a 'Double Double'.

The Lightweight gave a victorious debut to the Excelsior 'Mechanical Marvel', whose radial valves were operated by pairs of pushrods fore and aft of the

De Selby Hill Climb, 1933

Stanley approaching Clady Corner at end of Seven Mile Straight, UGP 1932

Stanley leads Senior TT

Taken from No 2 Signalling Station, Stanley waves at No 25 Tim Hunt leaving the pits (in white helmet)

Tim 3rd, Stanley 1st, Jimmy 2nd, Senior TT

Stanley after winning Senior TT

Stanley congratulates Charlie Manders, 3rd Lightweight TT

cylinders. The winner, Syd Gleave, raised the race record but failed to beat Handley's 1932 lap record on a Rudge. The race was marred by the death of Frank Longman who crashed approaching Ramsey.

From the Island the team travelled to Europe for the Dutch TT, the Swiss, French and Belgian Grand Prix's, resulting in three firsts, three seconds and two fastest laps for Stanley.

It is interesting to note that a double win at the Dutch TT and after sharing the total prize-money with team-mate Hunt the resulted payment was only £161 each.

The Swiss Grand Prix

THE course selected for the important Swiss event is tricky in the extreme; four slow corners and half-a-dozen fast bends have to be negotiated, whilst the many sharp gradients call for constant use of the gears. Such is the Berne circuit which has to be completed forty-four times in the Junior as well as in the Senior race—without doubt a searching test of mechanical efficiency and road-holding qualities.

In the Swiss race, as in each of the other International events, the competitors represented the cream of the world's racing men and motor cycles and in the two important classes—the 350 c.c. and 500 c.c.— there was only one official Norton entry.

The 25,000 spectators who witnessed the Junior event on Saturday, July 30th, were immediately thrilled when it was seen that a Swiss competitor riding a Continental made machine led the field on the first lap, but his triumph was short-lived, for Stanley Woods, who travelled to Switzerland alone, without taking even a pit attendant or mechanic, rode into the leading position. From that moment the Norton held the lead, the tortuous twists, turns and climbs of the circuit seemed to mean nothing to Stanley Woods, for the Norton rider flashed round the course with the regularity that is characteristic of the "Unapproachable." Nothing occurred to mar the splendid ride which gave Norton yet another notable victory at the record speed of 73.61 m.p.h.

Next day the Senior race was run before 65,000 enthusiastic spectators. In the third lap, Stanley Woods once again proved the speed of his Norton by jumping into first place. As on the previous day, the hazards of the course held no terrors for him, and he established a lead of four minutes over his nearest rival after five laps had been run, and soon put up what proved to be a record lap speed at 80.42 m.p.h. and finally completed the 206 miles at the wonderful average of 76.44 m.p.h.—amazing figures on such a course.

Thus once again Norton established a double victory and once again performed the feat *for the second year in succession*. And so whether conditions are favourable or unfavourable—Norton mounted riders maintain their winning sequence with ease. The machine that enables such feats to be performed must be super-efficient in design and in construction— must, in fact, be "Unapproachable." Especially so when it is remembered that Woods collected these machines in Brussels after the Belgian Grand Prix, there being no time available to return them to the works even for inspection.

Woods, the only official Norton entrant in the Swiss Grand Prix, won both Senior and Junior events.

THE UNAPPROACHABLE **Norton** BEST TRADE MARK

1933 Junior T.T. Race I.O.M.

B.T.H. Magnetos.	20	0	0
Castrol Oil	120	0	0
Dunlop Tyres	120	0	0
" Saddles	20	0	0
Pratts Petrol	15	0	0
Tecalamit Greasers	25	0	0
Amal. Carbs.	35	0	0
Renold Chains	30	0	0
Well Worthy Rings	18	0	0
John Bull	3	3	0
Lodge Plugs	80	0	0
£	483	3	0

1933 Senior T.T. Race. I.O.M.

B.T.H. Magnetos	25	0	0
Castrol Oil.	128	0	0
Dunlop Tyres	175	0	0
" Saddles.	20	0	0
Pratts Petrol	15	0	0
Tecalamit Greasers	25	0	0
Amal Carbs.	35	0	0
Renold Chains	31	10	0
Wellworthy Rings	15	0	0
John Bull	3	3	0
Lodge Plugs.	100	0	0
£	572	13	0

Big reduction in earnings and no bonuses from Norton

Stanley winning 500cc Class ,Dutch TT

Stanley, Double Winner, Dutch TT

UGP 12th August

The twelfth annual Ulster Grand Prix motorcycle race was decided over the famous Clady circuit. From its small beginnings in 1922, the event had steadily grown until it was recognised as the fastest race in the world, second only in its importance to the Auto-Cycle Union's Tourist Trophy races in the Isle of Man.

It should be borne in mind that the Ulster Grand Prix in those days comprised a series of races within a race, with three scratch races and three handicap races run in conjunction, that is a handicap and a scratch race in the 250cc, the 350cc and the 500cc respectively, there was also a Governor's Trophy, a sealed handicap prize.

When Stanley arrived in Belfast for the 'Ulster', he was met by Joe Craig, who announced some bad news, Tim Hunt was to win in the forthcoming race, Stanley protested and explained that he had an agreement with Mansell back in the spring, to the effect that he would have a free hand in what would be his home Grand Prix.

Next morning Mansell arrived at the hotel and requested a meeting with Woods saying *"I believe that you are being awkward"*

Stanley reminded him of their agreement, but his reply was that if Stanley did not stick to the plan, that it would be his last race for Norton.

Stanley had to think very hard about the situation that he faced, for Norton were one of the very few competitive machines around and had been over the previous couple of years.

On race day reports came along that around the course generally, there was a good distribution of spectators, especially at Clady corner.

Stanley decided to go fast in the early stages and possibly break the lap record a few times, then slow down so that it was obvious to the spectators as to what was going on. However, things rarely go to plan. He was first away in the mass start, had a great lead at Aldergrove, well ahead at the Rectory corner he over-did things and grazing a straw mattress. When he went to change up, he found that his gearlever was bent in the opposite direction, he braked hard, jumped off and with his foot, forced the lever back and was away before anyone caught him. The race turned out to be a tough one, with both him and Hunt posting a joint fastest lap.

When Stanley came in to refuel, Craig advised him that Hunt was in trouble and to *"Keep as he was going"*.

He had, of course, won the 500 Class of the GP in 1930, 31, 32 and he didn't disappoint the fans either that day, making it four in a row, a wonderful achievement, despite an intermitting misfire having developed. Victory was not assured until he crossed the finishing line, hotly pursued by Walter Rusk, the Belfast favourite,

Stanley leading

Stanley the winner through the finishing straight

Senior Ulster Grand Prix.

Joint a/c. P. Hunt & self.   1st & 4th

Dunlop Tyres	£68	0	0
Amal. Carbs.	7	10	0
Lodge Plugs	24	0	0
Pratts Petrol	5	0	0
Castrol Oil	40	0	0

2/ £144 . 10 . 0

72 . 5 . 0

Prize Money   12 . 0 . 0

£ 84 . 5 . 0

riding for the Norton Team for the first time and Ernie Nott (Rudge) third. Hunt finished fourth with a broken steering damper.

SWEDISH GRAND PRIX

The Grand Prix of Europe was run in conjunction with the Swedish Grand Prix at Saxtorp on 3rd September. It was Stanley's first visit to that country and destined to be his last appearance on a Norton. The course was a nine mile triangular circuit, three miles of perfect Macadam; the remainder consisted of loose sand with cinders at a small section just before the start. S. Woods and P. Hunt were there to contest the 500 class and the three practice mornings were pretty hectic between learning the course and the technique of Sand and Dirt-track riding on a road racing machine. They both discovered the secret of controlling their speed in these conditions, but their times were still a few seconds slower than the V-Twin Husqvarna which had a greater turn of speed than the Nortons. They were then told that the 'Huskies' would

Swedish Motor Club

GRAND PRIX OF EUROPE FOR MOTORCYCLES

SEPT. 3rd, 1933

ENTRY FORM.

Ank. 28. JUL. 1933

Besv.

(Please use one form for each cycle)

The undersigned hereby confirms having taken notice of the "Special Regulations", valid for the GRAND PRIX OF EUROPE 33, and will accept these regulations.

I hereby make entry in the speed event in the Class C 500 c.c. of one motorcycle as per the following statement:

Motorcycle-mark: NORTON   Number of Cyl. one

Make of engine: NORTON   Cyl. capacity 490 c.c.

Stroke: 100   „ diameter 79

DRIVER: S. Woods, 2 St. Thomas's Road,

Mount Merrion Estate, Blackrock, Co. Dublin

„ License No. S.C.8. issued by M.C.U.I.

ENTRANT: Norton Motors Ltd,

Bracebridge Street, Birmingham 6.

„ License No. Z.412 issued by A.C.U.

July   the 26th 1933

NORTON MOTORS LTD.

(Signature of entrant)

Managing Director

Fees stipulated:
Entry fee .... Kr. 75:—
Premium for accident-insurance „ 75:—
Addition for traffic-insurance „ 15:—
Deposit for numberplates ... „ 10:—
in all Kr. 175:—
enclosed.

Entries to be sent to:
Grand Prix of Europe,
P. O. B. 138.

Malmö.
Sweden.

N. B. — No entry will be accepted unless accompanied by fees stipulated!

---

in 'close order', they overtook a slow Swedish rider in a' different race', Erik Lundburg, who was riding a 250 FN.

Sunnqvist shut off, Stanley and Tim swerved from behind him to take the lead, Sunnqvist had passed on the left of Lundburg at well over one hundred mph, Stanley, closely followed by Tim, passed on the right. Sunnqvist startled Lundburg with his unexpected passing and he swerved violently to his right, missing Stanley and colliding with Tim Hunt. Lundburg was killed outright and Tim suffered concussion and a badly shattered leg, so bad that he never raced again.

Sunnqvist was now in the lead, Stanley now riding alone would have no hope of catching him until he stopped to refuel after fifteen laps. Sunnqvist was to find that his 'quick filling' tank had not been filled up and was delayed more than three and a half minutes, although, unaware of this, Stanley was still driving his machine hard. At the end of the sixteenth lap, he received a signal from his pit and misread it. Nortons' used a small blackboard on which was chalked an arrow, if it was inclined upwards, meant more speed required, horizontal meant all is well and when the arrow was downwards they were to slow up a little.

The pitman in the excitement of the moment, instead of giving him the slow signal seemed to be holding the board with the arrow horizontal. On the seventeenth lap he received no signals at all, as the pit crew believed that he had received the slow down signal and were looking at

only stop once for fuel, while the Nortons' would have to stop twice.

The race was run in perfect weather over thirty laps before a colossal crowd estimated at over 100,000. Woods and Hunt went to the start-line with the only instructions, *"Win if you can"*, but right from the start the local rider Rangar Sunnqvist took the lead. After a mile or so there was an S-bend, Sunnqvist got his line wrong and the Nortons' seemed to gain a few yards, this cost him the lead. On the straights Sunnqvist would regain the lead, with the Nortons' over-revving in his slipstream and this went on for eleven laps. When the Nortons' refuelled at the end of the 12th lap, Sunnqvist got the lead again.

A couple of laps later, the Norton men caught up with him. Three machines riding

Stanley with Nystrom Brothers, Norton agents Sweden

Stanley Woods, No. 5, start of the 500 race

their stopwatches to see how much he had eased. Next lap, Joe Craig was out of the pit signing him to slow down, he eased off at once but the terrific strain he had put on the motor in those hectic one hundred and sixty odd miles proved too much and the damage had already been done. At about half way round the next lap the

engine expired, big-end failure, a very unusual occurrence for Norton. Sunnqvist eventually retired with a broken chain and Gunar Kalen, who had overcome earlier problems, won the race.

There was considerable opposition to road racing in Sweden, for by then they expected to race over fully surfaced roads. The reason for the sand, cinder, macadam course was because of the climate in Sweden.

Gunnar Kalén prepares his Husqvarna 500 for the long race ahead

STANLEY'S WORDS THE REASON FOR LEAVING NORTON

"Many people have often thought and said that the greatest mistake I made was when I left Norton at the end of 1933, at that time I was undoubtedly the most successful road racing man in the world, I won the Junior and Senior TT's at record speed in both 1932 and '33 seasons and in addition innumerable continental races. The stage had been reached where the public were beginning to say Woods Norton, rather than Norton Woods, this didn't suit Norton Motors, they had four first class riders and if they could have wins every weekend with different riders, it

would have been much better publicity. As it was Woods was getting more than his fair share of publicity, from their point of view. The result was that the Norton team had to ride to 'Orders', which also meant sharing prize-money and all that sort of thing, which to a professional rider that I was, was not very satisfactory. We had a bit of an argument towards the end of the 1933 season and it was quite obvious to me that there was no future for me with Norton. I would win my percentage of races in the year and the cash return of racing was very small, for instance, the last international race I won was the UGP in 1939, 350 class, 1st prize was £12; you couldn't even get a good lunch for that nowadays. (£12 was the prize money from the Ulster Motorcycle Club)

The tale of how I came to be approached by the Vacuum Oil Co (Mobil Oil) is quite amusing, their trade representative in the Isle of Man was one of the most charming men that I have ever met, called Stafford May. In 1933, he brought over a young assistant, who knew nothing about the sport and after a few days in the Isle of Man, Stafford May realised that the young man needed a car in order to make contact with the various contacts in the racing stables, so he hired a car from the Athol garage, and I remember the day he took delivery, around midday. It was a beautiful June day and I was lounging up against the pillars of the Castle Mona Hotel when young Bert Perkins, that was his name drove up in his newly acquired car, stepped out slamming the door nonchalantly behind him, walked over towards me, I could see smoke coming out from under the bonnet and I said "Bert would you not put the fire out before you leave the car". Panic stations immediately, he hadn't a clue what to do, so I lifted the bonnet, disconnected the battery and the flames died down, it wasn't flames, just the wiring. He went to the hotel, got on the phone and read the 'Riot Act'. They got another car within minutes, these were not very prosperous days and nowadays you couldn't get a replacement car if you paid in gold, it was simple enough anyway. Bert and I struck up quite a friendship, later on that year, an inter-company agreement which governed the

Stanley in 1980 reviewing his personal 1930s Moto Guzzi correspondence with Manxman Tom Shimmin

payment of retaining fees to racing motorcyclists, had fallen out amongst themselves, it turned out to be a free for all. Their directors were having a meeting amongst themselves, they had signed up the Husqvarna Company to use their oil, not only in the racing motorcycles but in the factory. It was quite a big contract and they thought they had the freedom to pay any sum they wanted to motorcyclists, they should really do something about it.

Stafford May said, "Well if we are going to race we need to get somebody of the standard of Stanley Woods".

WE DO NOT HOLD OURSELVES RESPONSIBLE FOR LOSSES OR DAMAGE RESULTING FROM DELAY IN FILLING ORDERS
CAUSED BY STORM, STRIKES, FIRE, DIFFERENCES WITH WORKMEN OR ANY CAUSE BEYOND OUR CONTROL

Vacuum Oil Company, Limited

MANUFACTURERS AND MARKETERS OF HIGH GRADE LUBRICATING OILS AND GREASES
SOLE MARKETERS OF Mobiloil - THE WORLD'S QUALITY MOTOR OIL

TELEGRAPHIC ADDRESS
VACUUM, PHONE, LONDON.
TELEPHONE
WHITEHALL 1010 (14 LINES)

WHEN TELEPHONING PLEASE ASK
FOR EXTENSION Nº _____

GARGOYLE

MANUFACTURING PLANTS,
WANDSWORTH, LONDON.
WEST FLOAT, BIRKENHEAD.

BRANCH OFFICES

BELFAST
SCOTTISH PROVIDENT BUILDINGS.
TELEGRAMS VACUUM

BIRMINGHAM
9, CAROLINE STREET.
TELEGRAMS VACUUMPAN

BRISTOL
55, QUEEN'S ROAD, CLIFTON.
TELEGRAMS GARGOYLE PHONE

CARDIFF
DOMINIONS HOUSE, QUEEN STREET.
TELEGRAMS VACUUM

DUBLIN
32, NASSAU STREET.
TELEGRAMS VACUUM

GLASGOW
400 E, CATHEDRAL STREET.
TELEGRAMS VACUUMPAN

HULL
27, SCALE LANE.
TELEGRAMS VACUUM

LIVERPOOL
CUNARD BUILDING.
TELEGRAMS VACUUM

MANCHESTER
196, DEANSGATE.
TELEGRAMS VACUUM

NEWCASTLE-ON-TYNE
COMMERCIAL UNION BUILDINGS, PILGRIM STREET.
TELEGRAMS VACUUM

SHEFFIELD
QUEEN'S BUILDINGS,
QUEEN STREET.
TELEGRAMS VACUUM

UNLESS STATED OTHERWISE, ALL
OILS ARE QUOTED AND INVOICED
PER UNIT GALLON OF 9-LBS.

ALL QUOTATIONS ARE WITHOUT
ENGAGEMENT UNLESS STATED OTHERWISE.

AUTOMOTIVE LUBRICANTS DEPARTMENT.

CAXTON HOUSE, WESTMINSTER,

LONDON, S.W.I.

IN REPLY
PLEASE REFER TO
B1/COMPS.

3rd January, 1934.

Stanley Woods, Esq.,
  Mount Merrion Park,
    Blackrock,
      Co. Dublin.

Dear Mr. Woods,

We have pleasure in enclosing herewith
a cheque payable to you for the sum of £1,500.

This represents payment of the retaining
fee in accordance with the terms of the Competition
Agreement you have signed with us for 1934.

It is most gratifying to have the
pleasure of co-operating with you and we sincerely hope that you will have a successful season
so that the arrangement will prove to be to our
mutual advantage.

Yours faithfully,

VACUUM OIL COMPANY, LTD.

Competitions Division

AEP/SGT.

Another director said, "Well, there in no chance of getting Stanley Woods, he is Castrol and Norton. It was young Bert Perkins who said in his ignorance, "Has anyone asked Stanley Woods"?

It was of course realised that no one had asked so they passed the ball to Bert, "Would you like to ask him", Bert replied, "Why not".

He sent me a telegram to know would I give him an interview with a view to a change. I can't remember how he worded it, but in those days, to send a telegram, 6 words were one shilling (5p), you could pre-pay a reply, the telegram was delivered to your house, then the boy would take the answer back, I replied, "Yes". Another telegram came back, could I give an appointment arranged for a couple days later, he came over to Dublin, I met him in Dunlaoire, off the Mail-boat, after breakfast he put the proposition to me and I said I would consider it, I then took him down to Dublin. I lived about 4 or 5 miles out in the suburbs from Dublin and introduced him to every Dublin rider, of any prospects or hope, including Tyrell Smith, Charlie Manders and Tom Byrne and we signed them all up for Mobil Oil.

We finally got home, I gave him an option on myself for a figure which was considerably more than we settled for, which was more than I had earned in a whole year with Norton, winning most of the races and that's the way I came to change. I must add that it changed my whole way of life, my whole outlook on racing and changed everything for the better.

After the season ended I was approached by the Vacuum Oil Company with a view to riding the Husqvarna machine, I had already an established and friendly relationship, purely social with the Moto Guzzi concern and when Mobil came up with the Husqvarna offer and a retaining fee which was exactly five times greater than that paid by Castrol. I couldn't resist it because I had seen the Husqvarna in action a month earlier in the Swedish GP, I knew they had the speed and could see they handled well and I made the decision to leave, a mistake that I have never regretted, the combination of Woods Husqvarna, Woods Guzzi or Woods Velocette, my name was always on top".

NEGOTIATIONS FOR 1934 SEASON

At the 1933 Motorcycle Show in London, always held in November, he announced his decision to Bill Mansell, feeling that his position within the team had became untenable. His former boss wished him well, but did not hold out much hope for him as there were very few competitive machines around. Norton, who were undoubtedly the most enthusiastic of the manufacturers had over the years, produced an evolving series of great racing motorcycles. Stanley had been staying at the Royal Palace Hotel in Kensington during the show period when he wrote to Moto Guzzi, requesting the use of one of their works 250s for the 1934 Lightweight TT. They could not believe their luck in getting a rider with an already established reputation and he must have been their first foreign and most famous signature up to that point. Enrico Parodi, whose brother Giorgio was one of the founders along with Carlo Guzzi, had been an admirer having met Stanley socially on the Island in 1933.

Back then Terzo Bandini was entered for the TT by Moto Guzzi and Enrico had offered Woods a spare 250, if he could get Norton to agree for him to ride in the Lightweight as well, but the company would have none of that; another little known reason why he had become so disillusioned with Norton. The agreement duly arrived at the Royal Palace Hotel, as he had used their note paper and was forwarded on to his home in Dublin.

It took the form of a blank contract, for him to fill in his own terms, signed by Giorgio's father Emanuele Vittorio Parodi (who had put up the initial capital to start the company). Stanley was also looking for a 350, he had approached Velocette at the show but his suggestions were turned down. Instead he entered into a tentative agreement with one of the Collier Brothers at Matchless. In their Plumstead workshops, the Colliers had revived the Cammy AJS in 350 and 500 form, this design, which had come with the Wolverhampton assets to Woolwich when the two companies merged in 1931 and were hoping to make a come back to racing. Stanley made three trips to London, at his own expense, taking the 350 out on the road for testing, but each time returned with it on the train.

Chapter Six
1934-1935

STANLEY AND GEORGE ROWLEY were entered in the North West 200 (May 12th) on a pair of AJS ohc 350's. Stanley had endless trouble in practice, including a damaged petrol tank and George sportingly offered him his machine for the race, but Stanley retired with gearbox trouble - it was the last straw. The company had already entered him in the Junior TT, but he refused to ride it, claiming that the model had poor performance and reliability and that it would be very bad publicity for him and indeed to the Company, for him to ride such a machine. He never received a penny for all his work and expense, nor would they listen to any advice.

In their verbal agreement there was a sum agreed, it was construed by them as 'after development and riding', but Stanley's understanding of their agreement was 'after development and if suitable would ride'.

In January he had travelled to the Moto Guzzi factory situated at Mandello Del Lario on the shores of Lake Como, (stunningly beautiful

area thirty five miles north east of Milan) to test their 250 and 500 race models. The day after his arrival he was surprised to learn that he was also expected to ride for publicity purposes on the last leg of the Rosa d'Inverno (Winter Rose), Italy's big winter rally on 15th January from the factory to its finish in Milan.

The weather in Northern Italy in January was bitterly cold, but as he had come out equipped with leathers, he had no hesitation in taking part and did not find the cold too trying. At the finish in Milan the city was blanketed in freezing fog and the scenes were amazing. Many who had ridden from the most distant parts of the country were bordering on collapse, all were cold and hungry. Arrangements had been made by the various Italian manufacturers to cater for their riders and machines. Stanley accompanied the Guzzi directors to their main agent, where they were all entertained with plenty of food, wine and a big warm fire. A trophy was awarded to the manufacturer with the highest figure of merit; this was arrived at by a formula based on the number of entries and the mileage covered, of the 3000 machines entered that year, 733 were Moto Guzzi.

The next day it was sunny but cold and it was time to try out the 250 single and the 500 bicilindrica, both were race ready with open exhaust pipes.

The testing was carried out on the open roads skirting the edge of Lake

Mandello Del Lario, January 1934

97

Rosa d' Inverno with Enrico Parodi

Como in the direction of Chiavenna and the Swiss border which was only 40 miles away. His first impressions were more favourable towards the 250 but found the gear change a little difficult he recommended changes to gear ratios and brakes.

Carlo Guzzi, the designer agreed to put them in hand

250 Guzzi

by Jock Leyden

at once and would have them ready for a try out at the Grand Prix of Barcelona at the end of April. At this point Stanley left for home, thanking Giorgio Parodi and Carlo Guzzi for all their kindness and generosity during his stay.

Giorgio was born in Venice in 1897; his family had a flourishing shipping business at Genoa. He was a pilot and on leaving the Italian Air force after the First World War, with a loan of 2000 lira from his father, he founded the 'Moto Guzzi' with his mechanic Carlo Guzzi at Mandello in 1921, at the young age of 24.

The Parodi family were the only share holders in the company; Carlo Guzzi the designer was paid a royalty on production. In mid April it had been arranged for Stanley to return to Italy, to Monza track on the outskirts of Milan for another test session before proceeding to Spain. The lightweight was to his liking, apart from the gear change, which was still difficult and uncertain.

The 500 left a lot of room for improvement, with its slightly longer wheelbase than his last season's Norton

Giorgio Parodi on Moto Guzzi Sport 15

April 22nd 1934

Grand Prix of Barcelona.
1st 250 c.c. & 500 c.c.

Prize money 500 c.c. Pts. 4000
    "   "   250 c.c. "   750
Vacuum   500 c.c. "   1000
    "   250 c.c. "   750
Appearance Money   " 3000 £250.0.0
Moto-Guzzi S.A.   £ 50.0.0
                          £ 300.0.0

explained to him that they were not sure about the contents of the box, so he had it opened for them and it was replaced, minus two sprockets. He never worried about the rest of the spares, perhaps they are still in Spain!

The sprockets made a big difference, but he would have been happier with an even lower gear on the 500. Giorgio Parodi had come from Genoa to see him ride but had to return before the end of the meeting. Stanley took the lead at the start of the Lightweight race and held it, winning by over a minute from Guigilielmo Sandri on a similar machine; however he still found the gear change difficult.

and he could not treat some of the tight corners in the manner that he was used to. The next weekend was spent at the home of the Parodi family at Genoa while the machines went back to Mandello for their final check. The bikes were sent by rail to Genoa and picked up by Stanley where he accompanied them along the Riviera to Spain. His first thought on arrival in Barcelona was to get out around the very twisty two mile circuit situated within the city boundaries in Montjuich Park.

A complete range of spares had been forwarded to Spain in order to save delay, but despite all his papers being in order, he was unable to get delivery of the box, so the first practice period had to be completed with TT gear ratios and the need for lower gears was obvious. The next morning Stanley, accompanied by an interpreter, went to the docks. They approached a foreman checker and

Aboard Rigid 500cc Mot Guzzi Bicilindrica

Giorgio Parodi was overjoyed at his success on the 250 and was confident that he would win on the 500. Stanley did not feel all that confident, for he found the five-hundred tough going on the short, twisty circuit and could only use top gear once per lap and only for about a quarter of a mile. Local rider Fernando Aranda had won the 350 class on a Velocette and entered it in the big class, taking the lead and setting a very hot pace. Stanley was in fourth place and after about ten laps was second, having caught Aranda, but try as he would, he could not pass him.

As the race reached the half distance mark he became desperate, Giorgio Parodi was about to leave for his train. He had Aranda and Guzzi thoroughly summed up, he made his move on the bends after the pits and got past him with nothing to spare, only to have him re-pass on the braking for the hairpin. Disappointed he decided to make another effort and on giving her all she had, passed him once more. Having got the lead, he would have to try and keep it, but by now well beyond the safety limits, he knew that if things continued it could only lead to disaster. Woods slowed to about the speed that Aranda had been setting and the latter made no effort to pass him, so Stanley won the race by just over thirty seconds. His average speed for the big race was only three miles an hour faster than his speed on the

Ice Race, Sweden

lightweight, fifty eight compared with fifty five miles per hour, which gives a fair indication of the type of course and the unsuitability of the five hundred.

Next day he delivered the two machines back to Moto Guzzi and reported on their performances. He travelled to Berlin and the Avus Track to test the Husqvarna and after that he returned to Ireland looking forward to his next outing on the 250 Guzzi.

There were many changes to be made to the Husqvarna machines before the start of the racing season, Stanley was invited to Sweden in February where he took part in an Ice-race at Vallentuna on a machine lent by Rangar Sunnqvist.

At the Avus track near Berlin these early tests of the TT model left him quite happy with the handling of the machines.

Weeks before the Isle of Man races a canvas backed lorry containing the Husqvarna racing bikes and spares was being hoisted aboard a ship at Gothenburg, when a

Leinster 200

Lorry with bikes at Gothenburg Harbour

chain broke and the lorry was dropped from a considerable height into the hold of the ship. It finished upside down on top of its precious contents. The battered and bent machines were rushed back to the factory where rapid repairs were carried out and the bikes only just arrived at the Island in time for the first morning's practice.

The big news for the 1934 TT was that Stanley would be riding Guzzi and Husqvarna machines. Out came the headlines, "Foreign racing challenge", "British road race supremacy in jeopardy", "Prospect of defeat in our own TT this year".

Stanley himself thought that he was past what was a reasonable age for a racing motorcyclist.

After the Spanish event there was only a week or so to the start of practising in the Isle of Man. For publicity purposes for Husqvarna, he was up early and was first on the line, being the previous year's winner had the honour of 'First Off' in TT practice and had the freedom of a clear road. All went well for the first eight miles or so when coming round a fast bend just after Ballacraine, on peak in third gear, he found a shepherd with a flock of about twenty sheep on the road. He shot through the flock, glancing off a couple of them but came to no harm, however he decided that it would be wiser to ease back a bit and let some other rider lead the way.

For another ten or twelve miles everything was perfect, then as he braked for Sulby Bridge the down tube of the frame broke, this made her very unsteady in the steering and as it had also happened during the tests on the ice, it should have been a warning to them. Bringing the bike back to Douglas by lorry, he soon had

Stanley with Husqvarna Ice Racer

Ernie Knott, Kalen and Stanley

her stripped and proceeded to strengthen and repair the frame with strips of 1"x1/8" mild steel welded each side of the down tube of the frame, so that he could go out

Discussing carburation

and practice the next morning.

The 'Huskie' had the speed but they were dogged by bad luck throughout the practice period. It also had high fuel consumption and kept oiling plugs, the cause of the latter being that the Husqvarna was not fitted with oil-control rings. Stanley had access to a big lathe in the workshop at the Manx Electric Railway depot but as he was running out of time, he only managed to fit the rings to the rear cylinder. During the whole practice period he was unable to cover even a single flying lap and in fact he never put in a lap above 60 mph, while the lap record stood at about 83 mph.

He stated that he would not feel really at home on the Husqvarna until he had done three or four laps non-stop, how right this was proved to be. When Folke Mannerstedt (the designer) arrived on the Island he insisted that the machine be fitted with a new frame, Woods was happy with what he had and much more time was wasted.

Carburation had always been a problem, but at the last moment, just before 'weighing in' on the day before the race, they overcame the last of their troubles, although this upped the fuel consumption fractionally.

The day of the race brought low visibility, rain and wet roads not a very encouraging prospect after his experiences in practice.

PRACTICE PERIOD 1934

One morning he encountered some trouble on his first practice lap, just before Sulby Crossroads, after finding that he could not affect repairs, pushed the machine a few yards to the Sulby Glen Hotel.

Anxious to get the bike parked safely, knocking on the side gate, the proprietor invited him in for a cup of tea and enquired why he had not stopped before. Stanley replied, *"I have never broken down here before"*.

On entering the dining room, he recognized many well known riders, including the whole Triumph team at breakfast. At first he seemed surprised, then a few minutes later, a racing bike stopped outside and another rider appeared and was greeted by the owner,

Mannerstedt, Kalen, Woods and Knott

ten minutes later a couple more. They stopped for anything up to half an hour, then left, knowing they could reach the start-line and get in one more lap before the roads opened.

It had always been Stanley's policy to put in as many continuous practice laps as possible, by being up early, on the line, complete two laps and be well into the third before the roads were opened. Practice periods were

Sulby village in 1934 with famous phone box in foreground and Sulby Glen Hotel

invaluable for showing up any weak points in the machine that sometimes could be rectified before the event.

JUNIOR TT

Guthrie won the Junior TT at a record speed of 79.16 mph with a fastest lap of 80.11 mph, a new record for a 350. Guthrie had the use of Stanley's signal staff as he was not riding, due to his difficulties with AJS. Norton were anxious for Simpson to win, as he was due to retire at the end of the year, but Simpson finished second, nine seconds astern of the winner, with Nott third on the Husqvarna.

LIGHTWEIGHT TT

The Lightweight Moto Guzzi, by contrast proved most satisfactory and in the first practice session knocked 20 seconds of the existing lap record. They arrived on the Island with, in addition to the race bike, another with experimental constant-mesh gearbox. After more tests on both, he was convinced that this arrangement was a big improvement on the old one, which gave endless trouble with jumping out of gear, even though the experimental unit was supposed to be fractionally slower than the race machine.

All Moto Guzzis from the beginning had unit construction engines and the gears within the crankcases, one circuit of oil for everything. As the new constant-mesh gears appeared to absorb more oil than the older cluster, this meant less oil circulation at the top end of the engine, now, on the initial tests at the factory, there had been a tendency for the engine to seize, this had been solved by increased piston clearance.

On the Sunday before race week, it was decided that the two machines should be tested against each other to determine the performance of both in acceleration and maximum speed. This was carried out on a quiet stretch of road near the Point of Ayre on the northern top of the island. By dusk they had the new model running well and there was practically nothing to choose between them in overall performance.

Returning to their hotel that night, delighted with the results of their tests, the head mechanic insisted that he would have to strip the engine for examination before the race, which wasn't until the following Wednesday, so he would have plenty of time.

Next day Stanley went off to watch the Junior race and it was only just before Tuesday's weigh-in, that he was told that the Guzzi mechanic had swapped over the cylinder, piston, head and cam-gear of the older engine to the new crank-case, in an effort to get that little bit more speed that he thought that the old engine possessed. Now of course the increased piston clearance

Carlo Agostini alias iL Moretto one of the first Moto Guzzi employees, later the famous foreman mechanic in the 'Race Shop'

Graham Walker, having ridden for about 6½ laps in close company with him, he was riding one of the winning Rudges".

The 1934 Lightweight race was won by Jimmie Simpson, who headed a trio of radial engined Rudges.

It was Simpsons only TT race victory, winning from team mates Ernie Nott and Graham Walker taking 2nd and 3rd places. During the first lap of the race, Sid Crabtree, winner of the 1929 Lightweight race, crashed in foggy conditions near the Stonebreakers hut on the mountain section and was killed.

SENIOR TT

During the Senior race the Husqvarna's handling was impressive, it went where it was pointed and stayed on line. At the end of the first lap Stanley was second to Jimmy Guthrie on his Norton and on the third and fourth laps made fastest lap of the race. Then on the last lap at the Mountain Box and still holding second place within ten miles of the finish, Stanley ran out of petrol when he had three minutes in hand over the third man. If he had had more high speed non-stop laps during practice and had known the petrol consumption, things might have been different.

STANLEY'S WORDS
GREATEST MISTAKE DUTCH TT JULY 1934

"Like most people that do anything, sometimes they usually make a mistake and the man who never made a mistake never made anything. I came to the conclusion that my fall in the first lap, in the Dutch TT on the Husqvarna in 1934 was probably the worst mistake I ever made. Normally I was a very good starter, but in that particular race, for some reason the machine did not get off

was absent, a fact that was unfortunately over looked with the inevitable ending.

STANLEY'S WORDS

"I went to the Isle of Man in 1934, confident of victory in the lightweight race on the Moto Guzzi, but due to the unfortunate decision of the head mechanic to make a last minute alteration in the machine that I was going to ride, it seized at Sulby on the very first lap, I got going again but at reduced speed and I finished in fourth place just behind

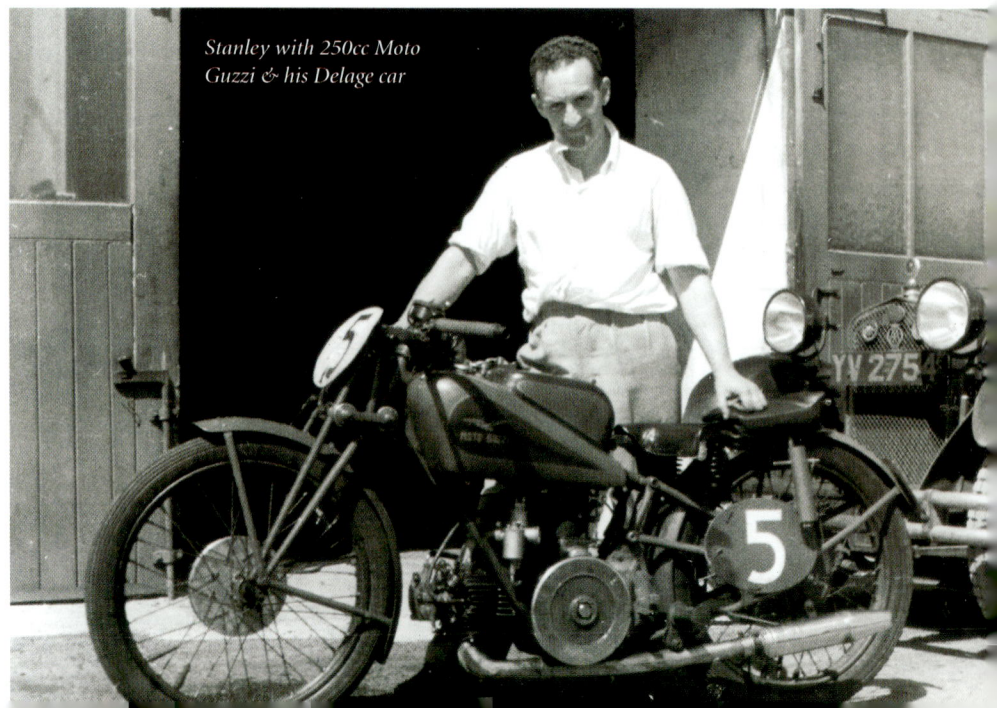

Stanley with 250cc Moto Guzzi & his Delage car

Start of Senior, Kalén (extreme right)

Last minute discussion with Mannerstedt

Stanley's 250 Guzzi passing No2 Signal Station Glencrutchery Road and St. Ninnan's Church

Governors Bridge

the line as well as it should, I won't say I was last, when we were about a third way around the course on the first lap I was ahead of the pack, overtaking the leaders very rapidly, a group of about six led by Jimmy Guthrie on a Norton.

I admit I must have misjudged the speed or something, I laid her down and the back wheel went into a slide, I steered her into it and by doing so I approached the outside edge, further than I meant to and had to lay her down again which started her sliding again. The back wheel hit the grass edge and the bike and I ended up at the bottom of a 6 or 8 feet ditch, I have complete memory and recall of the event, I was not knocked out and I was ok and to be candid I have never thought very much about that accident until I started to think about it in the last few days and I now think that the cause of the accident

The Husqvarna at speed approaching No 2 Signalling Station

Guthrie (Norton), Senior winner

Marie Louise aged 21

was that I was unable to practice at maximum speed.

When we arrived in Holland a week or ten days later we found that the fork spring had collapsed, now this must have happened sometime, possibly in the last lap in the Isle of Man, because I had not noticed any deterioration in the handling of the machine during the TT in which I was lying 2nd to Jimmy Guthrie but I ran out of petrol

Unfortunately we did not have a spare spring and I had to practice with the collapsed spring, with the result, I was not able to corner at anything like my maximum speed. The spare fork spring only arrived just in time for the race and looking back on it I know that quite apart from the fork spring trouble, with a lack of practice, I was probably in the height of high stress.

The last year before that race had been a year of excitement and stress, in the first place I had married a French girl which turned out to be a mistake, I took her home to her mother around about Easter and I had really

expected to meet her again later in the season but this did not happen.

Then on the Norton team we had no trouble mechanically or anything like that, we were unbeatable, one result of this supremacy of the Norton machines where we were not over stressed, we had the speed on the straights and though we did not loiter on the corners, we were never pressed, the result was that I had never taken this particular bend on the Assen circuit at maximum speed.

I had never approached it at truly "do or die speeds" and the speed of the Norton, which had increased probably the best part of 10 miles an hour over the previous 3 years and the Husqvarna was even faster, so I came into this bend at excessive speed and looking back on it, I think that it was possibly an error of judgment brought on by this element of stress, largely because quite apart from the fact that the Norton situation had deteriorated to such an extent that I left them at the end of 1933, so that really is the story of my worst mistake".

At the local hospital an X-ray revealed a broken scaphoid bone in his left wrist and was kept in plaster until after Christmas, for a while it was not expected that he would be able to ride again.

Insurance Compensation	£275. 0.0
Dutch Hospital less	10. 0.0
Doctors Fee	10. 5.0
X rays etc	60. 0.0
Insurance Agents Commission	2.15.0
	————
	£192.0.0

1935

Early March, this would be a month of excitement as Stanley prepared for his first trip outside of the continent of Europe, to the Grand Prix of Tripoli, to be run on the new Mellaha Circuit.

Breaking his journey, he joined the Parodi family again for a few days at their Genoa home before journeying on to Rome to meet three other riders. Arrangements had been made for them to travel from the coast near Rome to Tripoli by air in a flying boat of Italian origin, the flight across from Rome to Sicily, landing for fuel and lunch at the port of Syracuse, a brief halt, before the last leg of the flight to Tripoli.

Next morning after breakfast, they travelled to the circuit just outside the city. In an ultramodern setting, it's Grandstands, Timing box, Signalling tower and pits

were all in bright white concrete with fully grown palm trees everywhere, built regardless of cost by the Fascist Government.

Stanley had not ridden a racing motorcycle since parting company with the Husqvarna at about 110 mph, at the Dutch TT, 8 months earlier. When practice commenced, held on open roads, traffic was very light, a mixture mostly of camels, donkeys and the occasional motor vehicle.

During this first practice session he concentrated on getting the feel of the new spring frame of the 500 Moto Guzzi and getting all the controls adjusted to his liking. His wrist felt a lot better and by lunch time he had put in a lap at just under 100mph, which was just under the existing record. He liked the feel of the spring frame which seemed to handle a lot better than the old unsprung version, and in the afternoon session, pushed up the unofficial record to 104mph.

Over dinner that evening, with everyone now familiar with the new course, the talk generally was about speed, and as there was nothing like this event in Europe, the question was, how many machines would complete the distance.

The following morning saw more practising with official scrutiny in the afternoon, however, towards the end of practice the club informed him that there appeared to be some irregularity in his entry and that his name did not appear on the entry lists. This did not worry him too much as Giorgio Parodi was expected that evening in his private airplane and he would sort things out.

Parodi arrived late that afternoon and was greeted with the bad news, he said. *"Don't worry about anything, you and I are dining with the Governor, Marshal Balbo this evening and he will soon put things right"*

Over dinner, Balbo assured both that there was nothing to worry about at all and that he was as good as on the line. Next morning about an hour or so before starting time all seemed fine, but then a protest was lodged by Count Giovanni Bonmartini, who had entered two of his Rondine CAN (Swallow), DOHC supercharged transverse four cylinder machines which he had financed the development of. Marshall Balbo had threatened that he would not start the race if Stanley Woods was not allowed to ride, with only minutes to go the protest was upheld, the governor threw the starting flag on the ground and walked off, while Giorgio and Stanley pushed the spring frame Guzzi to the side.

Three of the rigid Guzzi models started, ridden by seasoned Italian riders, Omobono Tenni, Terzo Bandini, and Giordano Aldrighetti, but as the 25 lap race hotted

Marshall Balbo at Mellaha Circuit

GP Mellaha (Tripoli) eventual winner No 9 Tarruffi with mechanic Ciceroni and No 8 Amicare Rossetti (2nd)

Piero Taruffi Rondine) leaving the pits at Tripoli

up they all retired one by one. The lap record was hoisted to 108mph, with victory going to Piero Taruffi on a Rondine, with team mate Amilcare Rossetti runner up.

The performance of those machines was outstanding for their day; Gilera acquired the rights to the C.A.N. Rondine in 1936.

On the following Tuesday morning on presenting themselves at the airline office, it was found that they had one passenger too many. After a couple of abortive attempt to take off, the pilot returned to the landing stage. After much discussion they pumped off some fuel and next time they were successful and as they landed at Syracuse they discovered that they had a stowaway. A Guzzi mechanic had bribed one of the porters, borrowed his hat and overalls and had smuggled himself aboard and after more talk was allowed to continue. As the aircraft approached the coast near Rome the sea was found to be choppy, so they landed 40 miles up the coast - it was all part of the adventure in those days.

Back at Mandello his entry form was discovered in a drawer in Giorgio's office. It had been completed in Dublin, certified by the Motor Cycle Union of Ireland, where it had been sent for transit to the R.F.M.I. in Rome and had been over looked.

Italo Balbo was a founder member of the newly created National Fascist Party in 1921; in 1928 he became General of the Italian Air Force.

In July 1933, 24 Savoia Marchetti S55X flying boats under the command of General Balbo made the first transatlantic formation flight on a round-trip from Rome to the Century of Progress Exposition in Chicago. During Balbo's stay in America, President Franklin D Roosvelt invited him to the Whitehouse and presented him with the Distinguished Flying Cross, upon his return to Italy he was promoted Marshal of the Air-Force, after that the term 'Balbo' entered common usage to describe a large formation of aircraft.

In November 1933, Balbo was appointed Governor General of the Italian colony of Libya; however there was bad blood between Mussolini and the flamboyant Air Marshal. In 1939 Balbo publicly criticized Mussolini's support for Adolf Hitler after the German invasion of Poland, and on 28th June 1940, Balbo's plane; a Savoia Marchetti SM79, was shot down by Italian gunners over Tobruk and he was killed. The Italian government maintained that the incident was an accident of friendly fire, but family and friends strongly believed that it was an assassination on Mussolini's orders.

VELOCETTE 1935

It was only after arriving in the Island when one of the Velocette team, a rising star H.E. Newman, went down

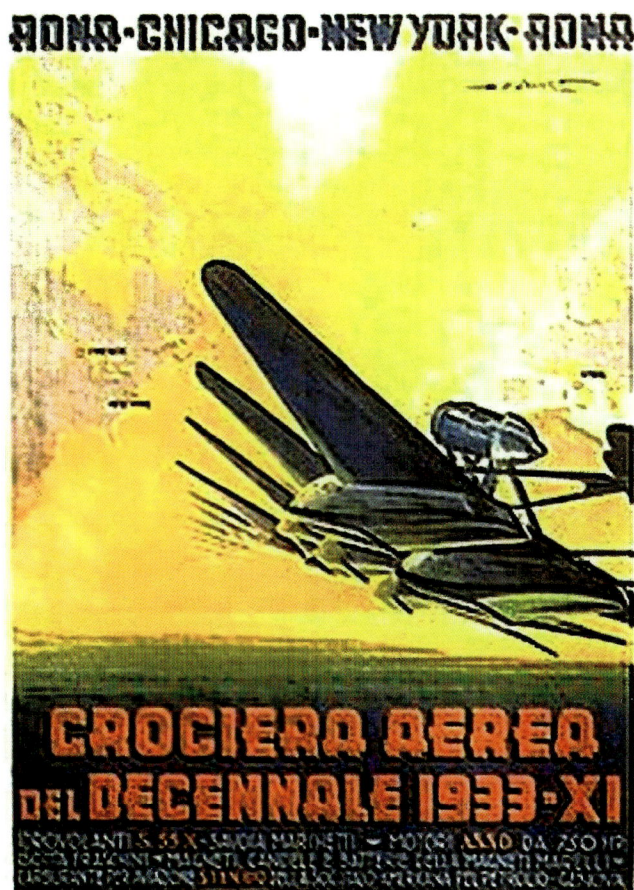

Poster for Balbo's Transatlantic flight

with pneumonia, that Stanley approached Veloce once more, to have a 350 ready for him on the first practice morning, so that he could qualify for the 'Junior' and evaluate it for them. He had always thought that they had potential but was politely turned down again. Later Stanley found out when talking to Joe Craig, that it was Walter Handley, their star rider, who did not want him on the team. It was towards the end of practice that he learned that Handley had been involved in an accident and would be unable to ride. Within minutes, he was approached by Percy Goodman and asked to take over his entry in the Junior TT. Stanley consulted with Giorgio Parodi and talked about the prospect of riding the Velo, Giorgio's only reply was, *"How much are they going to pay you"*?

With time for only one lap, he agreed to try the machine, completing the lap at 73 mph, 5 seconds slower than the fastest Norton. He was convinced that the engine was a winner but condemned the machine on grounds of its uncertain steering, with the rear wheel stepping out on high speed bends when speeds approached the 'century mark', brakes almost non-existent by the standards that he was used to, wrong gear ratios and he decided not to ride it.

LIGHTWEIGHT TT

The Lightweight race was run in less than ideal conditions, at the start the mountain mist was down as far as Signpost Corner, about 2 miles from the finish. The 24 year run of British victories was about to be broken Stanley led throughout on his Guzzi, setting the new record lap at 74.19 mph, but it was this bad visibility that caused his stable mate, Italian champion Omobono Tenni to crash at Creg-ny-ba on his 5th lap. Tyrell Smith (Rudge) and Ernie Nott (Rudge) were 2nd and 3rd. It was a first TT victory for a continental manufacturer; in addition Stanley, Tyrell Smith and Gordon Burney (Moto Guzzi) 8th Place took the Club Team Prize for the Leinster Motorcycle Club.

The win was an easy one, but upon examination of his engine it was revealed that if he wished to complete the course in the Senior, he would have to change his way of driving as it had been his policy to drive her to the maximum 7,700 rpm in the intermediate gears and cruise on top. As he shut-off over the finishing line in the Lightweight, the engine broke. It had always been his practice to shut-off and coast to a stand-still and push the bike back, so that they could examine the machine after 260 odd racing miles.

One of the mechanics, stripping the machine for the examiners noticed a hole in the top of the cam box and put his hand over the end of the rev-counter drive, to hide it. While the press took photographs, a rocker arm roller had fractured, increasing the tappet clearance somewhat and the arm had come out through the alloy cam box. These very same components, only doubled up, were used on the 500 engines.

SENIOR TT

The Senior TT was one of the most remarkable races in Isle of Man TT history, when Stanley scored an impressive victory and broke the British domination of the Blue Ribbon of motorcycling, bringing his Moto Guzzi into 1st place, with a record breaking victory by 4 seconds and creating a sensation.

He had failed to finish in both races that he had started on the 500 Moto Guzzi machine prior to the TT that year, the Barcelona GP and the Northwest 200. The cause was usually engine failure and this had dampened his hopes with regard to any TT success. With only weeks to go Guzzi set out to modify the offending parts and also took the opportunity to reduce the power output by lowering the compression ratio a little. But would the modified motor stand up to the thrashing of a seven lap Senior TT?

Tenni at Majestic Hotel

During practice on this fine handling machine, he soon found himself setting the pace like something of his old style. On the last morning of Senior practice he was out early with the race bike, riding one lap to bed in the chain and brakes, also trying out a six gallon petrol tank, (An amount that would have a detrimental effect on the handling when full).

At the end of that lap an Italian mechanic met him just past the finishing straight at St. Ninnians crossroads with another machine, all warmed up. They exchanged machines and he continued to practice. A sheet was thrown over the race machine and it was wheeled away and was not seen again until the day before the race. At the weigh-in, there was a great interest in the big red Guzzi, dubbed by the press as the 'Foreign Menace', but no one noticed the big petrol tank.

Later whilst Stanley was talking to Joe Craig, he remarked, *"The twins are fast but they are thirsty beasts,* Stanley's replied *"That's right"*.

Craig was convinced that the Guzzi must make a second pit stop, another Norton victory seemed assured.

It was the first year that a preliminary warm-up of engines was introduced and the Manx flag was used by the starter, instead of the Union Jack. With the dry roads and sun in places, the decision to postpone the race from Friday until Saturday for the very first time proved fully justified. Riders were dispatched at 30 second intervals and at 11.30 am Jimmy Guthrie, riding No.1 by virtue of his win the previous year, was on his way and setting a blistering pace. Stanley No. 30, seven times a TT winner, was out to repeat his victory of Wednesday and made another good start 14½ minutes after the leader.

At Sulby, Stanley got his first signal and was 15 seconds astern of the Flying Scotsman, by the end of the first lap; it had gone up to 28 seconds.

Stanley had miscalculated, he had based his scheme on Guthrie's 1934 winning speed, which had been run in the rain, and had forgotten that the Norton Ace had put in a practice lap of 27.1 minutes that year as well. Trying to save his engine, because of the earlier problem with the 250, he knew he must not flog the Guzzi.

On the next circuit, 11 seconds ahead of the third place man Walter Rusk (Norton), but was still 47 seconds behind the leader, as Guthrie had made record laps on his second and third laps. Now 52 seconds behind, on the fourth circuit the Guzzi got round at 27.22 minutes, against 27.32, the first time that he had travelled faster than the Norton, but his slight increase in

speed was partially camouflaged by a superb refuelling performance.

Lap five 42.5 seconds in arrears, it was essential that Guthrie should retain a cozy looking lead, another fast one for the Irish man 26.26 minutes, a record 85.66 mph and Guthrie's lead was now only 28 seconds with two laps to go. During the 'sixth' he made up another 3 seconds and at the end was only 26 seconds adrift. The Guzzi pit were seen to be getting ready for another fill-up and had clean goggles at the ready, but Marjorie Cottle, the famous lady trials rider, who was standing with Joe Craig, remarked to him,

"If Stanley is going to make another stop, why has one of his pit crew got the indicator boards at the ready, if he was to make a precautionary stop, they could tell him".
Norton had copied Stanley's earlier idea of having a second signalling station and just earlier, Joe had phoned their station at Ramsey to give Guthrie the 'go easy signal'. It was now too late for him to alter that direction.

At the start of his 7th lap Stanley was expected to stop but instead went flying straight through the finishing straight and now somehow, he had to claw back 26 seconds and if safety rev-limits couldn't do it, chances had to be taken. Once in practice he had

Stanley at weigh-in

Tyrell Smith (Rudge) Note: rev counter on side of petrol tank and alloy rims

Stanley faces time-keeper Ebblewhite

Stanley wipes his goggles at Cronk-na-Mona

Gordon Burney (250 Guzzi), Bradden Bridge

Stanley pushes off Senior Guzzi, Jack Williams No 35

carelessly missed a gear, let the engine shriek up to 9000 rpm and nothing snapped, so it was all or nothing.

On the run to Ramsey and over the mountain, using all his skill and daring to pull back the deficit, the spring frame of the Guzzi gave it much better road holding. He also let the engine run up to 8200 rpm at times from the Bungalow to the finish, without a sign of trouble.

He crossed the line at the very moment when Guthrie was being declared the winner.

JOCK LEYDEN TAKES UP THE STORY

"I remember that race very well, in fact, I'll never forget it. I had walked from the Press-box in Glencrutchery Road as far as Braddan Bridge, while the race was on, looking for things to draw and was walking back to the finish when the race ended. Stanley flew past me 'literally' as he took the jump on the rise (now known as Ago's Leap) and fled on to Quarter, I had seen Stanley many times, but not like this, he was right out of the saddle.

Stanley was in a real hurry this time but I knew he had no hope of clawing back 26 seconds from Jimmy G, in a lap. I continued on my way and arrived in the pits to see

that Jimmy Guthrie had finished and was already being proclaimed the winner, a huge Union Jack was being draped behind him – the foreign menace had been trounced once again.

A smiling Guthrie was seated on his mount, behind him a radiantly happy crowd – Norton directors, Gilbert Smith and Bill Mansell, with son Dennis, Joe Craig, race mechanics Bill and Frank, the victorious Oil Company rep and a host of well wishers and others, hoping to get in on the act. When the press photographers assembled they clicked their shutters, a mellow voice whispered in my ear, "They're wasting their time, Stanley's won", It was Harry Ryan, the Dunlop rep, how could I believe that?

Stanley was still out on the course, having started No.30, Guthrie started No.1 and was home after a 26 second lead going into the final lap, Stanley the winner?, impossible! But the roar from the spectators massed on the grand stand grew louder and then it exploded when Stanley crossed the line on his Guzzi. He had done the impossible, with a new record lap to win by just 4 seconds! Four seconds after over 3 hours racing. Historians say that the 1935 Senior TT produced the most exciting and

STANLEY WOODS WINNER SEN. T.T. 1935

Scene after 1935 Senior

dramatic finish in the long history of the race and I was there to see Stanley Woods win it". From 'Stanley Woods My Hero' by Jock Leyden

It is worthy of note that both winning Moto Guzzi's were fitted with spring frames, alloy rims and rev counters, a first since the inception of the event. This would have a profound effect on all motorcycle manufacturers.

Since 1926 Moto Guzzi had come to the Island, year after year with a machine that seemed like a certain winner, yet for one cause or another, failed to win. As they were a small company with no business interests in Britain it was more a personal ambition of it's directors than a sales effort.

Well content with their success winning the TT

Lightweight T.T.

1st Prize	paid.	£100 – 0 – 0
Moto Guzzi S.A.		300 – 0 – 0
Fastest Lap.		50 – 0 – 0
Emanuele Parodi.		100
Dunlop Tyres. paid		125 – 0 – 0
Vacuum Oil		70 – 0 – 0
Lodge Plugs pd.		50 – 0 – 0
Ferry Saddles. pd.		28 – 0 – 0
Shell Petrol paid		18 – 0 – 0
Ferodo Brakes paid.		33 – 0 – 0
Amal Carbs. paid		35 – 0 – 0
Bowdenex paid		5 – 0 – 0
A.C.U. Starting fee		30 – 0 – 0
Renold Chains paid		20 – 0 – 0
		£958 – 0 – 0

Senior T.T.

1st Prize	paid.	£120 – 0 – 0
Moto Guzzi S.A.		400 – 0 – 0
Fastest Lap.		75 – 0 – 0
Emanuele Parodi		200 – 0 – 0
Dunlop Tyres. paid		187 – 10 – 0
Vacuum Oil paid		120 – 0 – 0
Lodge Plugs paid.		100 – 0 – 0
Ferry Saddles pair.		25 – 0 – 0
Shell Petrol paid.		20 – 0 – 0
Practice Lap (Guzzi) pd.		25 – 0 – 0
Ferodo Brakes paid		50 – 0 – 0
Ferodo Statement paid		25 – 0 – 0
Amal Carbs. paid		35 – 0 – 0
Bowdenex paid		5 – 0 – 0
A.C.U. Starting fee		30 – 0 – 0
Renold Chains paid		50 – 0 – 0
		£1467 – 10 – 0

1935 – 500cc. 120° Twin MOTO-GUZZI the machine on which Stanley Woods won the SENIOR I.O.M.T.T. by 4 seconds after a record-breaking last lap.

Guthrie's Senior Norton by Jock Leyden

Lightweight and Senior Trophies and having achieved more than they had ever hoped, they decided to curtail their racing activities outside Italy.

With some persuasion they left a spare 500 with Stanley on the island so he could have a machine for the Ulster.

Only a week after the TT a letter dated 27th June arrived from Percy Goodman of Velocette, requesting a meeting.

Norton double TT Winner 1931-4 plus Junior TT 1935

TELEGRAMS:
VELOCE, BIRMINGHAM
CODES BENTLEY'S

TRADE MARKS.

REFERENCES

OURS   PJG/MH 27635

YOURS

The **Velocette** MOTOR CYCLE

MANUFACTURERS AND PATENTEES

VELOCE LIMITED
HALL GREEN WORKS · YORK RD
HALL GREEN · BIRMINGHAM (11)
CONSIGN ALL GOODS G.W.RY. TO HALL GREEN STATION.

TELEPHONE
SPRINGFIELD 1145
(PRIVATE BRANCH EXCHANGE)

Winner
of the
JUNIOR TT

1926·8·9.

27th June
1935

FIRST "350" MACHINE
TO COVER 100 MILES IN
1 HOUR.

1930
MANX GRAND PRIX.
1ST, 2ND, 3RD, 4TH, 5TH
6TH, 7TH, 8TH.

1929.
JUNIOR T.T.
1ST, 3RD, 5TH, 6TH, 7TH,
10TH AND 11TH.
FASTEST LAP. RECORD
TIME.
AMATEUR T.T.
1ST "350" CLASS.
SOUTH AFRICAN T.T.
JUNIOR RACE. 1ST & 2ND
UNLIMITED CLASS.
1ST AND 4TH.
AUSTRALIAN T.T. 1ST.
DUTCH T.T. 1ST.
FRENCH GRAND PRIX
1ST.
ALL JAPAN
CHAMPIONSHIP 1ST.

1928.
JUNIOR T.T.
1ST, 2ND AND 5TH, ALSO
60 WORLD'S RECORDS.

1927.
JUNIOR T.T. 2ND.
AMATEUR T.T.
1ST "350" CLASS
FRENCH GRAND PRIX
1ST.
CZECHO GRAND PRIX
1ST.

1926.
JUNIOR T.T.
1ST, 5TH, 9TH & TEAM PRIZE.
AMATEUR T.T.
1ST "350" CLASS.
BRITISH GRAND PRIX
1ST.
GERMAN GRAND PRIX
1ST.

Stanley Woods Esq.
Mount Merrion Park,
Blackrock
Co. Dublin.

Dear Sir,

After this years experience in the T.T. I feel
that we shall not do any good until we secure
the services of a rider such as yourself.
I should therefore like to discuss with you
(as soon as you are in a position to do so)
arrangements for next year.

We desire to discuss this as the earliest
possible moment so that we can take immediate
steps to develop a machine suitable for next
year.

We consider it necessary to have the assistance
of a rider like yourself in order to develop
the machine so that it will handle properly
on the course.

As soon as you have time I should be glad if
you would get into touch with me personally.

Yours faithfully,

P. J. Goodman

DUTCH TT

In early July he travelled to Holland to meet the Velocette team, during practice his first impressions of the 350 Velocette were confirmed, it had lots of speed, but nothing else had changed since his previous brief outing. Despite this, having made fastest lap in practice it gave him encouragement.

In the race itself he led the field for several laps until the machine began to lose speed, followed by a smoke screen, with the engine developing so little power he had to retire from the race. The cause of the trouble was the oil pump which was found to be full of sand, but where that came from was never explained.

Woods (Velocette) leads Richnow (350cc NSU)

GERMAN GRAND PRIX

For the first time since going free-lance, he found himself without a mount. Casting around for a suitable machine, he remembered that a New Imperial twin had lapped the TT course at over 80 mph in the hands of two different riders Sid Gleave and Ginger Wood. Stanley had some success with the marque in Ireland, and never a man to let "Old acquaintance be forgot", he approached his friend Norman Downs for the use of one of their 500's and arranged to ride it in the German and Belgium Grand Prix.

What he did not note, was that Gleave had crashed quite heavily in TT practice after having completed three laps at over eighty and in the Senior race Ginger Wood crashed on Lap 3 at Windy Corner.

From the first practice in Germany it was necessary to fight the machine the moment the power was turned on, due to the poor steering, and he had great difficulty in completing the necessary number of qualifying laps at the required average speed. The result was that he could not use anything like peak revs, had quite a lot of trouble with plugs and was a very happy and relieved rider, when this trouble overtook him in the early stages of the race. He did not proceed to Belgium but instead returned the model to Birmingham with comments and lukewarm thanks.

MORE ON THE NEW IMPERIAL

The original entry list for the 1935 Senior included Ginger Wood (New Imperial No.15), Doug Pirie (HRD Vincent) and Sid Gleave (New Imperial), Ginger and Sid were also entered in the Lightweight on New Imps and Pirie in the Junior on a Velocette. After Sid's practice crash, Pirie abandoned the Vincent Senior ride and took over both of his entries; Pirie had not originally been entered in the Lightweight.

In the Junior, Doug Pirie had a magnificent ride, coming in 4th behind Guthrie, Rusk and White on works Nortons and ahead of Nott, Ernie Thomas, Harold Daniell, Les Archer, Tyrell Smith and many other famous names. Sadly however, in Wednesday's Lightweight and after getting up to 6th on lap four, he crashed at the 33rd and was fatally injured.

Sid Gleave made a good if slow recovery and never raced again. During WW2 he served as an Air Transport Auxiliary delivery pilot and Avro test pilot, but the latter job proved fatal, as he crashed a new Lancaster on September 11th 1944 at Woodford near Coventry. Stanley "Ginger" Wood commenting years later about the handling of the New Imperial 500 Twin said that when riders such as himself made suggestions to a manufacturer they were ignored, but when his near name sake made suggestions, he got things done.

SWEDISH GP

His next appearance was in Sweden on the Husqvarna, since the previous year, the race team had incredible misfortune, Stanley's crash in the Dutch TT, then only eight days later, their star rider Swede Gunnar Kalén, lost his life in the German GP and a short time later in the Belgium GP, Aire van der Plugm, the Dutch agent for Husqvarna, who was riding as a private entry, collided with another rider and was killed.

People began to say that the Husqvarna was dangerous; Stanley disagreed, for he always took the blame for his crash in the previous year's Dutch TT.

In the spring of 1935, the directors decided to cease motorcycle production and concentrate on Husqvarna's sewing machines and other products.

For prestige reasons, Husqvarna agreed to support the 1935 GP only, with Stanley as their sole official entry, paying his own expenses to Sweden. During practice he found that the frame had been strengthened since the previous season and that she handled to perfection.

Stanley (No. 1) Ivar Skeppstedt (No. 2) and Michael Gayer (No. 3)

Woods (Husqvarna) in winning form, Saxtorp

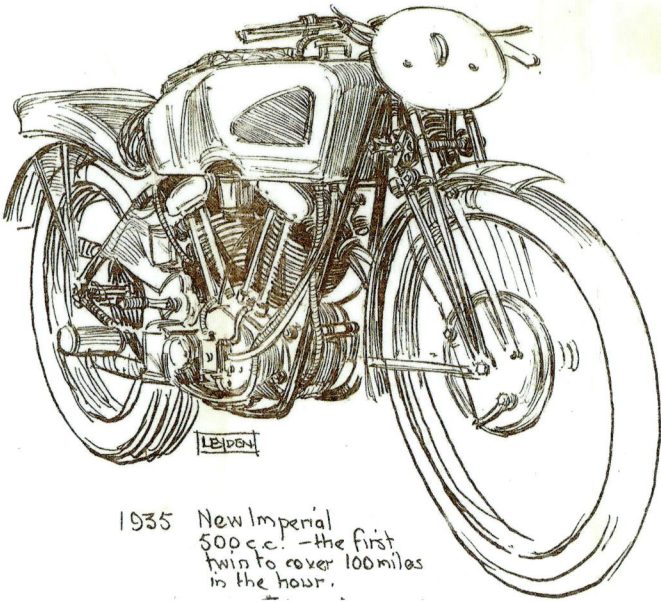

1935 New Imperial 500 c.c. – the first twin to cover 100 miles in the hour.

HUSQVARNA

1935 500 cc MOT-GZZ

Drawings by Jock Leyden

Despite gearbox trouble he won the 500 event, ahead of the Supercharged BMW's and DKWs.

Between June and August 1935, Stanley Woods had competed on racing 500 V-twins of three different manufacturers (Moto Guzzi, New Imperial and Husqvarna).

ULSTER GP

The last major race of the year was the European Grand Prix, "The Ulster", which had for the first time in the British Isles, the honour of staging the F.I.C.M. annual event 'The Grand Prix of Europe'.

The first practice revealed that the Guzzi twin was struggling to get within 200 revs of her normal 7,700 rpm. Mindful that on the Island he had to be careful not to let the motor run above this figure, one can imagine how disheartened he was in the race itself, he was able to stay reasonably near the leading bunch until on the 9th lap, suddenly, the Guzzi went on to one cylinder. The carburetor needle clip had broken, dropping the needle into the jet, it was a failure that turned a racing 500 into a 250 and the Amal people were unable to explain why.

Belfast man Bruce Hill a person friend of Walter Rusk recalled the story.

1935 was a good year for him as he and Jimmy Guthrie, riding to orders shared 1st and 2nd places in practically every race they entered. Joe Craig with the unselfish approval of Jimmy Guthrie arranged that Walter should win the 500 race, especially as this was on his home territory.

In fact Jimmy Guthrie 13 years Walter's senior jokingly said "Don't make the race too hard for the old Scot".

The routine had always been to make it look like a real race, passing and re-passing and finally whoever was selected to win finished a few yards ahead of the other. Both Jimmy and Walter were on their 3rd lap, well ahead of the field, perhaps

Walter Rusk and Joe Craig

500cc Moto Guzzi

Walter, Stanley and Jimmy

*too far ahead, Walter said he simply could not get past
Jimmy and had thought that perhaps a real scrap was
expected. So on this lap Walter was confident that as he
knew the course so well he could pass Jimmy on the S bends
at Aldergrove.*

*He tried it, got level with Jimmy, but as it was a
scorching day, hit a melted tar patch, both came off, Jimmy
continued but Walter's bike was damaged, he could not
continue and lost the race.*

*I asked him later did he ever speak to Jimmy about this
and he said "No, nor did Jimmy ever raise the matter with
me".*

*Suffice to say, Joe Craig was livid with Walter for
damaging the bike.*

*I also asked Walter did he think that Jimmy's bike was
faster but he rather gentlemanly said "No".*

Jimmy won the race with a new record lap of 95.35
mph.

One day, Stanley got a surprise letter from Italy; it
was from the National Fascist Party. Mussolini, a life
long motor sport enthusiast, was inviting Stanley Woods
to accept the title of "Cavelier della Rupublica" (Knight

of the Italian Republic), on account of his services to
their industry. This was just after the Abyssinian crisis
and Italy's unprovoked aggression on Africa's last
independent nation and member of the League of
Nations, the world was shocked and he was advised not
to accept.

It was in this year that Arthur Carroll, whose brilliant
design work had done so much for the Norton marque,
was killed in a car crash.

CARS

In the RIAC Limerick GP on Aug 5th, Stanley was
entered by Austin Motors to drive a works 750 but
retired with a blown head gasket. He also drove a 995
Adler in both the RAC Ards TT and at Phoenix Park in
September, and they also ended in retirement.

1935 was his year of highest earnings; he also got a
fine retainer from Austin Motors, for they must have
thought it good publicity to have such a famous
personality competing in one of their cars, even though
he only made one appearance for the company.

Austin Works 750, Limerick GP

VELOCETTE – STILL NOT SIGNED

Development engineer Harold Willis had been horrified at Stanley's analysis of the Velocette after only one lap during TT practice, as none of their other riders had ever complained. Willis thought that the engine should be moved back, in order to hold down the rear wheel, but Stanley thought it should be moved forward. Goodman knew that all was not well with the race models in the 'navigational department', for he had witnessed one of their leading riders struggling with one at the 13th milestone on the Mountain Course.

Goodman accepted Stanley's opinion and wanted him on the team, but while he agreed to ride for them in the 1936 season, he refused to sign a contract until his suggestions were incorporated.

After the 'Ulster', he spent some time at the factory, where Willis approached him with a suggested set of gear-ratios; he replied *They will do, as they are the same as used by Norton Motors*.

Machines with new frames for himself and Ernie Thomas were being prepared with their help, which included a series of tests late that year in the Isle of Man, when lead blocks were attached at the bottom of the front down-tube to prove his theory. The frame layout was modified and improved, a new steering head assembly was designed to enable the front down-tube to run as close as possible to the front mudguard and some sort of rear suspension would have to be adopted at his insistence.

New Velocette double overhead camshaft motor

The problem had been one of weight distribution and the result of all their experimental work was a very high standard of road holding and steering, which was aided by a new pivoted rear fork with Dowty Oleo-Pneumatic suspension (a development of aircraft landing gear where air was compressed on impact and movement hydraulically checked).

A double overhead camshaft motor had been developed during the off season when rev counters were fitted for the first time, and the 'new' Velocette was first shown to the racing public, in the Isle of Man in May 1936.

WHEN STANLEY FIRST met 20 year old Mildred Ross the previous year it was love at first sight, unfortunately, he was already married and there was no provision in the Irish Constitution for divorce. He decided to resolve the situation by travelling to London and flew to Paris, where it had been arranged for lawyers to have the marriage to the lady from Lyons, dissolved. In Early April he and Mildred drove to London, where they were married in a civil ceremony. The couple planned an extended honeymoon of almost four weeks, travelling by road in the Delage to several countries.

The first stage of this journey was through France and onto Kanderstey, Switzerland, which he had known from earlier skiing holidays. It was late in the season and the weather had changed, so they spent a week walking in the lowlands before driving down to the Riviera to watch the Monaco Grand Prix.

Ahead of schedule, they headed to Spain where it had been arranged to meet Ernie Thomas, who had agreed to bring out a pair of Velocettes for Stanley to ride in the Barcelona GP on April 26th. The 500 class provided him

500 Velocette at Berne with experimental lead block on frame down tube

with his first taste of victory on a Hall Green product and the trio, with the two Velos, travelled up to Berne for the Swiss GP in early May, though this resulted in another retirement with the 350 and a 6th place in the 500 class.

DKW 1936

In March, the press announced: "The German Auto Union company has engaged Stanley Woods, the famous Irish TT winner, to ride a 250 cc 'Auto Union' motorcycle in this year's Lightweight TT race in the Isle of Man. The machine will be the same as that with which German motorcyclists won eight international trophies during 1935".

Mildred Woods

500cc Velocette at speed Berne 1936

With Anglo-Italian relations strained, it put a temporary halt to their sporting activities, so Stanley had to look elsewhere for a competitive 250. He had been very impressed with the DKW and was invited to Chemnitz in Germany, for a meeting with Herr Prussing, the head of the racing department, with the view to entering one of their supercharged 250's in the lightweight TT and returned to Dublin, having acquired a 98 cc DKW trials machine.

Some of his friends laughed when they first saw the little machine, but when they were invited to try it, all were very impressed of how advanced it was, as two-stroke trials bikes were virtually unheard of then.

A close friend, Dr Joseph Horgan, a Surgeon from Cork, inquired about the possibility of riding a DKW in the Patland Cup Trial. Horgan, who had not ridden for several years, had won the Patland in 1930 and the Patland Novice award the previous year on Rudges.

The sensation of the Patland trial held on 15th February 1936, was that M J Horgan was riding the little German machine of less than 100 cc, in the 250 Class which seemed to rule out any possibility of success but he finished second and won the Tredagh Cup for visitors even though he lost a lot of time through breaking the chain.

In 1937 and again 1938, Horgan won 250 and a first class award. That DKW was the smallest machine ever used in the Patland and Horgan said that it was ideal for the course.

Dr Joseph Horgan (98cc DKW)

Billy Tiffin, Stanley, Ernie Tomas, H. E. Newman, Nursery Hotel, Onchan

JUNIOR TT

The 350 Velocette went well in practice in 1936 but failed to top the leader-board. Stanley was still hot favourite and it was rumoured that he was holding something back. Unfortunately, at Sulby, on the first lap of the Junior, the camshaft coupling sheared, putting him out of the running. After that and to Stanley's dismay, Harold Willis decided to drop the design and revert back to single-overhead camshaft. The double-overhead camshaft layout had been a logical development to succeed the Dog Kennel type engine that had been performing reliably for years but lacked that bit of extra edge. Veloce Ltd. had a very small budget for development and claimed that it had discontinued work on the DOHC engine because of insurmountable problems.

LIGHTWEIGHT TT

The DKW concern was the largest producer of motorcycles in the world building machines at the rate of 20,000 per year. They had agreed to pay Woods a £150 "Starting Fee" to ride their machine in the Lightweight TT and thought that they were paying him a fortune but he had received a cheque from Herbert Terrys that morning for £200 for using their valve-springs and saddles on the two Velocettes that he was also going to ride.

The DKW would be fitted with German accessories and not the companies that he was retained by, which meant no bonus payments on that occasion. Stanley jokingly suggested to DKW: *"Take off all your accessories and I will ride it for free"*, however he did manage to have a Terrys' saddle fitted.

The 1936 DKW was an exquisite piece of machinery but far too fiddlesome to keep tuned to racing pitch, as Woods was about to find out.

Mellors who finished 3rd on the rigid frame DOHC Velo

STANLEY'S WORDS - 1936 LIGHTWEIGHT TT

"It was reported in the Motorcycling and in general press that The Mountain had burnt up my screaming DKW. Not True! My trouble was an oiled up plug! It happened thus: Before the TT I rode the DKW in the Solitude Race at Stuttgart. So far as I was concerned it was a waste of time, for, although the other works entries ran faultlessly my machine suffered from persistent misfiring.

Later on we went to Nurbergring where my machine ran perfectly. I was warned however that I must not exceed 4,400 RPM. If I did, one of the nine reed valves between the supercharging piston and the crankcase would break. I was supposed to be able to feel when the engine was at peak, for no revolution counter was fitted! This was more than somewhat difficult for me, as during the last season virtually all my riding had been on Moto Guzzis.

Preparing for practise, Delage in background

On both 250 and 500cc machines, the normal peak revs were 7,700 and it did not seem to do any damage if this figure was exceeded. Revolution counters were fitted as they were on my 1936 Velocettes. The 350 ran to 7000 RPM and the 500 to 6000RPM, the 500 would not exceed this figure while on the 350, the valves floated above this figure – simple!

I begged Dr. Prussing to fit a rev counter, or a speedometer but he would not consider doing so.

By race day I was fairly confident that I could judge the right moment to change up, except on the Mountain Mile on Snaefel. On this stretch the engine reached peak revs on third gear so slowly that the only way to avoid trouble was to change into top gear early and let her 'slog'.

I started the race quite confident that I could win, if I had no trouble. At Sulby, my first signaling station, I got

the signal "first by seven seconds". This was not as big a lead as I had expected so I went a little faster for the rest of the lap, but not by any means extending myself or the bike. At the end of the lap, my first lap position at Sulby was confirmed, however I had to wait until Sulby to learn that the little bit extra had affected my position, Sulby signaled all well, first by 24 sec. So having found the correct speed to give me a comfortable lead, I maintained it.

At the end of the second lap I had established a lead of one minute and eighteen seconds and by Sulby I had extended it to one minute, thirty seconds. Then trouble! On the Mountain I oiled a plug; I had been driving hard enough to keep her warm on the long climb in third gear. A fast plug change, but by the end of the lap I had dropped back to second place, twenty five seconds behind Foster on his New Imperial.

Both Foster and I stopped for petrol at the end of the third lap, so the pit loss of time could be ignored, more or less, a few seconds either way would affect the result. Off again on the fourth lap but pushing my self that little bit nearer the limit on the bends and corners and knowing that I would have to get near the engine's danger zone in third on the Mountain Mile. By Sulby, I had regained the lead by five seconds and by the end of the lap led Foster by twenty seven seconds, including slowing down for a second pit stop, only a short fifteen seconds, enough however, to drop me back to second place, five seconds behind Foster at Sulby.

Nothing to worry about, I could still win by a minute, unless I had more trouble and that's just what happened, singing along on third towards the end of the Mountain Mile, she went flat, just off tune. By the end of the lap I was down to second place once more, thirty five seconds in arrears. On the last lap the trouble became progressively worse and at Sulby I was more than five minutes down, just before the top of the Mountain she ran out of fuel.

On the sixth lap on the Mountain Mile I must have exceeded the permitted 4400 RPM and have broken one or more of the reed valves, reducing the crankcase pressure and increasing the petrol consumption by blowing it through the carburetor. She was a lovely machine to ride and handled to perfection but I found the rigid frame and fairly small section tyres very tiring, although I did not become aware of this fatigue until after the race.

Due to the postponement of the race from Wednesday to Thursday, on account of the weather the weigh in for Friday's Senior race was postponed until early Friday morning and as I had another little job to do on my

Left, Eric Brown, Stanley's pit man, start Lightweight TT

Stanley (DKW) Governors Bridge

In 1936 Irode one like this ~ I led the 250 T.T. but had Trouble & finally retired on last lap when Second, Stanley Woods

Senior Velocette before the weigh in, I did not have time for a "post mortem". However they got the message and for the 1937, their race bikes were fitted with a rev counter and sprung frames"

THE 1936 SENIOR TT
THE MYSTERY MISFIRE

The Senior Velocette was a three year old single-cam motor housed in the latest sprung rolling chassis and practice times had shown that he would have to work hard from the fall of the flag. The Velocette engine design, with its dry-sump lubrication and pressure feed to the vertical shaft and cam-box was known to require an extended warm-up period to ease her up to an efficient working temperature, before it would rev to maximum.

Stanley would not find out until the day of the race just how many laps he would need to reach this

optimum temperature and this need for extended warming-up would impose limitations during the opening part of the race.

Starting five minutes ahead of Jimmy Guthrie and intent on trying to save every possible second, Stanley was full of confidence, but at the end of the first lap he was lying second by 19 seconds. Guthrie extended his lead to 27 seconds by the end of the second lap. With the engine now going better by the end of the third, this was confirmed by his signal stations, showing him to be reducing the gap every ½ lap, first 23 seconds, then 18 seconds and at Sulby on the 5th lap it was down to 15 seconds.

Over the mountain he caught up with another rider Ernie Nott (Rudge) and could not pass him for some distance. It was not until he passed his signalling station at Sulby on the 6th lap that he realised that he had lost about 10 seconds getting past Nott and had dropped to 25 seconds behind the leader. However, all was not lost

Stanley pushes off his Senior Velocette

Senior Velocette at speed approaching No. 2 Signal Station

and with the engine going better than ever, during the run from Keppel Gate to Craig-na-Baa the engine reached maximum for the first time, but it was then that the Velocette developed a misfire. Accelerating away from the Craig, there was no sign of the misfire but as soon as he drove her to peak revolutions in top, the trouble restarted, causing an immediate drop in RPM and necessitating a return to third gear. At that point the misfire would disappear and the motor would rev cleanly up to peak in third.

Despite time lost due to this mystery misfire, the 6th lap was his best of the race and was a new course record. At the end of the lap, the Norton pit were getting ready for another "top-up" for Guthrie, so the stage was set for another last lap struggle. The crowds were on their toes; for the lead had been only 22 seconds and Guthrie's stop must have whittled most of that away.

For Stanley, those last 500 revs would have come in useful towards the end of the race, but it was not to be. Generally, the Velocette ran perfectly on the last lap, except where the road would permit her to be revved towards maximum, and then the misfire would return. Approaching Sulby Crossroads for the last time he gave his signallers the thumbs-down signal and as he sped past they could hear the engine missing a beat.

Stanley finished 1st on the roads and this year it was his turn to wait, then Guthrie came flying through to beat him by 18 seconds and Stanley was the first to congratulate him.

The 1936 Senior TT would be the last one that Guthrie would ever finish and losing by such a narrow margin the previous year had robbed him of recording the first ever 'Senior Hat-trick' by a rider.

Stanley had the unique distinction of having made four successive Senior fastest laps on four different makes of machines, 82.74 mph (a record) for Norton in 1933, 80.49 mph for Husqvarna in 1934, 86.53 mph (record again) for Moto Guzzi in 1935 and 86.98 mph, (yet another record) for Velocette in 1936.

Back at Hall Green the 500 engine was subjected to all manner of tests but the misfire could not be found.

Stanley and Mildred at finish of race

AUTUMN

Donington Park had opened in 1931 and was a very popular race venue in the thirties.

One novel method that Woods used to convey machines to a circuit was to call at Velocette's factory in Hall Green, Birmingham and pick up two machines. Then, with the rear seats taken out of the Delage, the 350 would fit in the back with its front wheel removed and parked alongside. The 500 would be carried on the near-side running-board, strapped to the doors with its front wheel resting in the car's spare wheel-well of the front mudguard.

Stanley congratulates Jimmy, the Senior Winner

On 3rd August Stanley was in tip top form at Donington and took the 350cc honours but retired in the 500 class.

He was invited to Italy in late September, where he had been entered by Moto Guzzi in the GP Della Nazioni, (Grand Prix of Nations) at Monza. Whilst practising on the 500 cc wide angle twin, the front exhaust pipe came loose. As he approached a left-hand bank curve at about 120 mph, the pipe came in contact with the track and caused the rear wheel to step out. He managed to straighten her out, without any conscious effort, but just when he thought that he had recovered control, the overwhelming strain on the rear tyre pulled it off the rim, resulting in a heavy fall. Giorgio Parodi arranged a private ward for him in the local hospital in Milan, though he suffered only minor spinal injuries it required nearly two months in plaster and the Moto Guzzi was a complete write-off.

AUSTRALIA
WINTER 1936-1937

In November, Stanley and Mildred left England by sea on Aberdeen & Commonwealth Line via Malta, Port Said & Colombo on the long voyage to Australia, by the time he stepped aboard the liner he had fully recovered.

This would be a racing holiday as well as a sales promotion for Velocette. The plan was to compete in two race meetings, the first run in conjunction with the South Australian Centenary Races, on December 29th, 1936 and then onto the Australian TT at Phillip Island, Victoria, on January 25th, 1937.

The trip had been arranged by Mr. L G Parry, the Melbourne Velocette agent, together with his counterparts, Mr. Lu Borgelt of Adelaide and Mr. Percy Williams of P R Williams of Sydney, plus the South Australian Government had contributed towards their expenses.

Early in the trip Mildred was presented with a small Bell & Howell cine camera and Stanley a pocket-watch by Mr. Lu Borgelt.

They brought two racing Velocettes with them a 350 and a 500 both rigid frame SOHC "Dog Kennel" models that were to be left behind and raced afterwards as Velocette's contribution.

Outside Lu Borgeit motorcycle premises, Adelaide

Off to the races at Victor Harbour

After 350 race

The Centenary races were held on a 7.25 mile circuit near Victor Harbour, 50 miles from Adelaide. Riding the 350 Velocette, Stanley won the 75 miles Junior TT at 79.9 mph. The second race on the programme the Senior TT over 100 miles, was won by Australian champion Clem Foster (Norton). Stanley, riding the 350 Velocette after damage to his 500's engine in practice, was third but he succeeded in setting the fastest lap of the race at 89 mph.

At January's Phillip Island event, Stanley was again dominant in the 350 cc race, winning comfortably at 77.36 mph, from Norton-mounted Jimmy Pringle, who averaged 75.50 mph. Pringle, a leading Australian star, had little trouble winning the 500 cc race at 85.30 mph, from Clem Foster (Norton) with Stanley third on the 350 Velo.

While in Australia the couple travelled extensively, made guest appearances at several civic functions and motorcycle club dinners, as well as enjoying some sightseeing. Lu Borgelt was keen on the publicity value and was host to them for the three weeks they spent in Adelaide. On their return journey, they were able to leave the ship as it approached the Suez Canal, take a train sightseeing in Cairo, rejoining the boat at Port Said.

During her time in Australia, Mildred gave an interview on 10th December and she disclosed some interesting background information. She and her younger sister Nora were born in Toronto, Canada. Their father had served in the Canadian Army and was wounded during WW1 and the family had moved to

Stanley, Mildred and L.G. Perry, Melbourne Velocette agent after 500 Race

Civic Reception

Maps supplied by Vacuum Oil Company

Dublin when she was 8 yrs old. She had been interested in motorcycles and motorcycle racing before she met Stanley.

She was at home in Dublin preparing for their departure to Australia when Stanley crashed in Italy, in late September. He flew back and she nursed him at home for 3 weeks, but despite this accident she did not worry about him racing, saying: *"I have too much confidence in my husband's ability to be nervous about him"*.

Stanley revealed in one of his interviews that in 1922 he had once booked passage for Australia but changed his mind a few days before the ship sailed, when he received an offer from the Cotton Motor Co. to ride in the 1922 TT.

KEN KAVANAGH
NORTON & MOTO GUZZI STAR
"I was the greatest fan that Stanley ever had, I discovered him in 1938 when I entered into the Christian Brothers Technical College, I had just turned 14 and he was still everybody's interest, following his recent racing holiday to Australia. They referred to him as 'Sir Stanley Woods', yes the tale had got around that he was 'Sir' and we poor colonials believed it. Years later, I was taken on as an engineering apprentice and his name was always popping up, he was also known as Mr. Velocette. The people of the day did not know that he had also raced Norton, Husqvarna and Guzzi, in Australia, his name meant only one thing, Velocette".

After their successful Australian trip and a few weeks rest, the couple were planning a hectic programme for May, which included races in Ireland, England and Italy. By now Mildred was an accomplished timekeeper. Stanley was a non-starter in the Leinster 200 as his Velocette was not ready in time.

DONINGTON PARK RACES
Easter Monday
For this meeting riding the 500 Velo pulling a very low gear, after several laps just before the end of the straight as soon as the engine reached peak revs the misfiring started.

By chance he happened to look down through the gap between the nose of the saddle and the back of the

Stanley and Mildred at his pit with rigid 500cc SOHC Velocette Phillip Island

petrol tank, and could clearly see the petrol "boiling over" out of the float chamber.

On the next lap, just before reaching peak revs in top gear, he held the float chamber with his left hand to see if he could stop the vibration, suddenly the engine revs soared to maximum with no sign of misfiring. He did a few more laps, alternately holding the float chamber and leaving it alone and once and for all proved the cause of all the trouble. The float chamber had been mounted on the oil tank to isolate it from the vibration but it was found to be flexing. Velocette overcame the trouble by using thicker metal on the oil tank and no further trouble was experienced from this source.

Finishing 5th in the 500 race, having lost a lot of time, he was relieved to have found the trouble that cost him the Senior TT, eight months earlier.

It was Coronation year, but for the North of Ireland Motor Club, the organizing body of the North West 200, it was a difficult one. The Ministry of Home Affairs presented them with an ultimatum, that unless there was unlimited insurance cover for spectators, permission to close the roads for the race would not be granted.

The Northern Ireland Government's action was taken in light of an unfortunate accident where many spectators lost their lives the previous season in the RAC Car TT, over the old Ards Circuit.

The province of Ulster was the only part of the United Kingdom where public roads could be officially closed for racing. At first it seemed to the organizers of

both car and motorcycle events, that the government was asking the impossible and the only outcome would be the end of both forms of sport in the province. With the race to take place on May 8th, a conference was held between officials of the club and the Ministry of Home Affairs. The Ministry stressed that it was anxious that the best possible arrangements be made to safeguard the public in the event of an accident. Protracted negotiations were completed with Lloyds of London to the satisfaction of the Ministry, for insurance cover of £100,000 per accident and £50,000 per rider, per accident.

The North West 200 was the first race in the world to have such colossal insurance cover, on the 55 riders it totalled £8,250,000.

As Jimmy Guthrie crossed the line to win his fourth successive 500 cc race at the North West 200 he got a great cheer, for he had equalled the record of Ernie Nott. This had been no walk over for Jimmy, for Stanley on the Senior Velocette led the first seven of the eighteen laps. He fell off on the eighth lap and damaged his brakes and Guthrie and White got ahead. After pulling into the pits Woods resumed, but finally gave up on the eleventh lap, which was a great disappointment to the thousands of spectators.

The Coronation Grand Prix, at Crystal Palace on the outskirts of London was the inaugural race meeting at the new two mile track, held on the 15th of May. During the Senior race, Harold Daniel and Jock West, were both

Stanley (Junior Velocette) rounds Governors

ahead of Stanley riding very hard. With the TT just weeks away, he decided to leave them to it as he never took chances; after all the TT meant everything to a manufacturer. Jock overdid things, came off early in the race and Harold had a massive slide, shedding his brake-rod, five laps from the end of the 30 lap race. He managed to recover the machine and to just stay in front of Stanley for the distance. Jock West remounted and came third.

Following their Coronation Tour, Stanley and Mildred were invited to spend a few days at the Parodi home at Genoa, for he had been entered by Moto Guzzi at the nearby Circuito Della Surperba to ride their 250. It was his first appearance there, winning the 250 class, beating the 350 record, then rode the same two-fifty in the 500cc race and finished third, behind the half-litre Guzzis' of Nello Pagani and Omobono Tenni.

One event he regretted never having entered was the Circuito Del Lario (known as the Italian TT), over the hilly twisting roads around Lake Como.

1937 TT

With the DOHC engines being dropped because of the failure in 1936, Veloce had obtained the sole rights to use a patented rotary-valve design that could be developed and which, it was alleged, produced some unheard of figure for a 350. Harold Willis was convinced that a race engine could be ready for the TT, but after some months

they realised that the new rotary-valve engines were not reliable and gave no more power than the poppet-valve types.

This only resulted in delaying development of the new single overhead camshaft, square-fin engines for 1937, which did not produce the required BHP figures, and Stanley could only finish fourth.

The tide had been slowly turning against the British lightweight, although Excelsior kept the flag flying for a while. Stanley returned on a Moto Guzzi and had a fierce battle with the DKW of Ewald Kluge. After Kluge retired, he looked a likely winner and led until the end of the fifth lap, now half a minute ahead of his team-mate. On the sixth lap, a misfire developed and by the start of the seventh and final lap, Tenni was leading Woods by well over a minute. Woods retired at Sulby with valve-spring trouble and Omobono Tenni completed his historic victory, in record time, to become the first Italian to win a TT, with Ginger Wood (Excelsior) in second place, in front of Ernie Thomas (DKW).

Stanley discusses his bikes with Harold Willis, Nursery Hotel

One day during Senior practice, Stanley saw Omobono Tenni stopped with Amal Carburettor personnel, trying to convey some problem to them. Knowing neither of them spoke the others language, Stanley, who spoke fluent Italian, realised what might be wrong. Having parked his Velocette, he offered to take the Guzzi for a lap and report back to them. Apart from solving the carburation problem, he found the Guzzi to feel large, compared to his Velocette.

The 1937 Senior TT saw the TT debut of BMW with English rider Jock West as their sole entry. Jock had to practice on a rigid framed model (which he claimed was hard work), until the spring–framed tele-forked machine arrived.

Just before the start BMW had urged him with 'What ever you do always try and finish'.

Stanley with his Senior Velocette

After a terrific struggle with the leaders, his petrol tank developed a very small crack. On the 4th lap he ran out of petrol, pushed to the pits from Cronk-ny-Mona, refuelled and again at the end of the 6th lap, to finish in sixth place at an average of 81.50 mph. West commented afterwards that BMW always put castor oil in the petrol to lubricate the supercharger otherwise the leak would have been worse.

For the next two Grand Prix events, the Swiss and German, Stanley would be Guzzi mounted. It must be remembered, that with the exception of Norton Motors, no British firm of motorcycle manufacturers were regularly entering a team for various continental races.

Stanley Woods

F.I.M.I.

81 BRIGHT ROAD,
DOWNPATRICK BT30 8LT
NORTHERN IRELAND

Senior T T Race 1937.

Stanley Woods personal record.

10.29AM. On the line. Happy, confident but not too optimistic!

11.30AM Jimmy Guthrie No.1 starts 90 seconds ahead of me. By Sulby, about 20 miles I'll know what to expect!

11.14.10AM Sulby – 10 seconds down on Guthrie

11.27.36AM Stand. Full report from Sulby. Frith & I dead heat.

11.34.54AM Sulby. 1st lap results. Third to Guthrie & Frith from there on forget the time and concentrate on getting there faster than ever

2nd lap. Second to Jimmy G but 7 secs ahead of Frith.

3rd lap. Still second, & still 7 seconds ahead of Frith – we both lapped in 25M 34S.

4th lap. Still Second to Jimmy G. but now 50sec ahead. Frith refilled at the end of 3rd lap.

5th lap Leading Frith by 10 seconds. Jimmy retired on fourth lap & I refuelled at the end of 4th.

6th lap Frith & I dead heat! I'm at my limit!

7th lap Frith breaks lap record and beats me by 15 seconds!
I had a wild slide at full revs in 3rd gear at the left hand bend after Ballig. – so called Dorans. When the geese stopped walking over my grave I knew I was going over my limit & calmed it a bit! Frith was reported to have had quite a number of hectic moments! So, a good young un is better than an old one!

Handwritten report of the 1937 Senior TT

Freddy Firth, winner of the 1937 Senior TT

Jock West (BMW) at weigh-in

Jock pushes in from Cronk-na-Mona

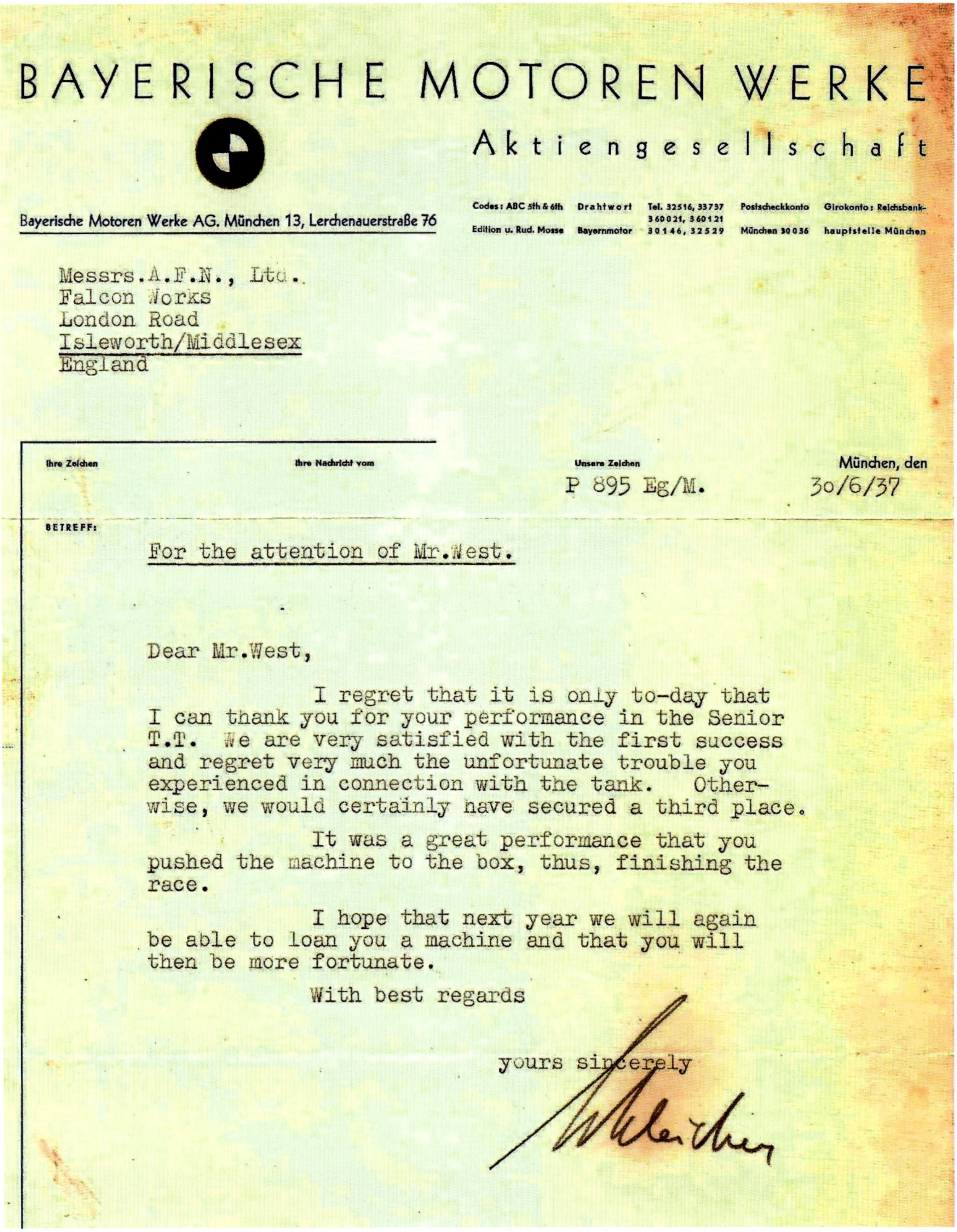

BAYERISCHE MOTOREN WERKE

Aktiengesellschaft

Bayerische Motoren Werke AG. München 13, Lerchenauerstraße 76

Codes: ABC 5th & 6th	Drahtwort	Tel. 32516, 33737	Postscheckkonto	Girokonto: Reichsbank-
Edition u. Rud. Mosse	Bayernmotor	3 6 0 0 21, 3 6 0 1 21	München 30 036	hauptstelle München
		30146, 32529		

Messrs.A.F.N., Ltd.
Falcon Works
London Road
Isleworth/Middlesex
England

Ihre Zeichen	Ihre Nachricht vom	Unsere Zeichen	München, den
		P 895 Eg/M.	30/6/37

BETREFF:

For the attention of Mr.West.

Dear Mr.West,

      I regret that it is only to-day that
I can thank you for your performance in the Senior
T.T. We are very satisfied with the first success
and regret very much the unfortunate trouble you
experienced in connection with the tank. Otherwise, we would certainly have secured a third place.

      It was a great performance that you
pushed the machine to the box, thus, finishing the
race.

      I hope that next year we will again
be able to loan you a machine and that you will
then be more fortunate.

      With best regards

yours sincerely

SWISS GP 3-4th JULY

The Swiss GP held in Berne, was the Grand Prix of Europe and the most important race of the year. The 250 promised to be a battle between two and four stroke machines, with the three factory DKWs' of Ewald Kluge, Walfried Winkler, Hans Hausler and the three Guzzis' of Stanley Woods, Omobono Tenni and Nello Pagani. Tenni led the DKWs' of Kluge and Winkler for most of the race, with Stanley and Pagani swapping fourth place, then on the 25th lap Stanley stopped at his pit and lost three minutes.

With the other two Guzzis' scheduled to run non-stop and the faster but more thirstier DKWs' stopping for fuel, Tenni won from Pagani, with Kluge 3rd, Winkler 4th and Stanley 5th having been lapped by Tenni, on the last lap.

In the Senior race the following day, Karl Gall's BMW took an early lead right from the start. Jimmie Guthrie and Freddie Frith soon got the measure of the twisty Bremgarden circuit and passed him. Gall retired on the 4th lap, next it was the 'blown' Gilera-Rondine of Giordano Aldrighetti, who chased for two laps until he stopped. Tenni took over third spot, with Stanley passing Otto Ley, leaving the British riders finishing 1st and 2nd, with Guthrie 2.5 seconds ahead of Frith and Tenni, Stanley finished 4th, 38 seconds behind his team-mate.

Whilst still on the continent, Stanley got a telegram from his mother, to inform him of the sudden death of his father. Edward H Woods, aged 65, had been hit by a car while he was out cycling on 23rd July 1937 and died the following day in Royal City of Dublin Hospital. Stanley was able to fly home for the funeral. The accident happened on the Stillorgan Rd - at that time Stanley lived nearby at Mount Merrion Park, Co Dublin.

GERMAN GP SUNDAY 8th AUGUST

The German Grand Prix was held over the difficult, rectangular five mile circuit at The Sachsenring, Saxony. Germany by then was deeply involved in international motor-sport and its people were pinning their hopes on their BMW, NSU and DKW riders.

In terrific heat a vast crowd of 250,000 were distributed around the course, in many places packed three and four deep. After a poor start, Jimmy soon established a comfortable lead and his third consecutive German Grand Prix victory was in sight. On the last

Stanley with 500 Bicilindrica

Ted Woods

corner of the last lap, not a mile from the finish line, where the Union flag was being hoisted, he crashed heavily. Gallant Jimmy Guthrie was taken to a local hospital in Chemnitz, where he died a few hours later.

The shock of his death reverberated around the world, for this 40 year old Scot, six times a TT winner, the upholder of his country's honour and prestige in foreign lands, had won the admiration of fans everywhere. Those fans knew they would never see his like again. Never before in the history of motorcycle racing, had such a famous rider been killed at the height of his success. Away from the track, he was a quiet, unassuming family man, who in partnership with his brother, Archie, ran their motor business in the border town of Hawick.

A guard of honour from the local N.S.K.K. was posted in the room where he died and many hundreds of people who had watched him that day filed past to pay their last homage until arrangements could be made to transport his remains to his home in Scotland.

At his funeral in Hawick, Craig, Stanley and other team members were among the pallbearers, with the Union Flag that the race officials at the German GP had been waiting to raise, draped over his coffin.

Jimmy Guthrie on that fateful day

There were several theories surrounding his death – that he had been forced off the track by another rider whom he was overtaking – that one of the lugs retaining the rear wheel had fractured – the rear axle had failed catapulting him into the trees - the conrod was also found to have broken or perhaps the engine had run low on oil (Norton's were known to use a lot of oil) and had seized throwing the machine into and uncontrollable skid.

Stanley was deeply effected by the death of his friend and said *"I did not really get to know Guthrie well until he joined the Norton Team but from that time we were close friends, our friendship grew in the following years when we were members of the same team and in the four season since I left the Norton Team. It will always remain one of my fondest memories that our rivalry in those years when*

Mildred, Jimmy Guthrie & Freddie Frith in the pits at German GP

we were the keenest opponents of one another never interfered with our personal relations. To the day of his death Jimmy Guthrie was the staunch friend I made when I first 'palled up' with him in 1928"

Even as late as 1989 he would never be drawn on the subject and just before filming began for the BBC documentary 'Stanley Woods the Movie' he was asked if he would speak about the Guthrie crash, but he refused. Three years later living alone with his two beloved cats he decided to speak of the events of July 1937 and said *"I had retired from the race, my machine had run out of petrol and I was free-wheeling down a gentle slope when a German and Jimmy passed me, the other rider being lapped forced Jimmy off the track into a line of young trees.*

As a mark of respect for Jim's memory, Norton withdrew its entries from the Ulster Grand Prix, won by Jock West, (BMW), after Stanley (Velocette) had retired from the lead with engine trouble, Ted Mellors, (Velocette) won the 350 class and Ernie Thomas, (DKW), took the 250 award.

TRIALS WINTER 1937-38
In the winter 1937-38, Stanley returned to trials riding. It had been a means of keeping fit all year round and the wetter, the rougher, and the tougher, the more he seemed to enjoy it. Now entered on a Royal Enfield, (his brother-in-law Gordon Burney was a partner in the importers 'Burney

Bush Cup winner, November 1937

'Hillberry', Burney's home, Mount Merrion, Dublin

Brothers'), with OHV engines, they were light and had plenty of ground clearance. Winning the Bush Cup Trial in November, the event starting and finishing in Enniskerry, Co Wicklow, in early 1938, he scored a second in Ulster's toughest trial, The Hurst Cup. Then in February he pulled off the unique feat of winning the Patland Cup for the fifth time. Later, a first in the McCrum Trial, demonstrated that he had not lost any of his old form.

1938 RACING SEASON

At the first road race of the season, The Leinster 200 at Tallaght, Co Wicklow on 7th May, Stanley won the 350 class with fastest lap on a Works Velocette fitted with a KTT motor.

'Hillberry', February 1938, 5th Patland Cup Winning machine

NORTH WEST 200

1938 saw more development in the organization of the North West 200; the North of Ireland Motor Club had been contributing towards the promotion of the event. Entries fees included insurance and for the first time entitled cross channel riders to three days hotel accommodation, Eire riders to two days and Northern Ireland riders to one day free, at the clubs expense.

There were also three distinct handicap awards, one in each class, plus an award in each class for the best performance on handicap by a first time competitor. The scheme proved popular and entries soared, they totalled seventy, comprised of eighteen 500s, thirty three 350s and nineteen 250s.

Manx Grand Prix riders were able, through a special concession, to ride side by side with 'Works' riders and not have their amateur status affected. The club had yet another innovation which helped both riders and spectators, the race distance of eighteen laps of the eleven mile circuit would be reduced for the Junior race by one lap and the Lightweight machines by two laps. This arrangement proved popular with riders and 'brought in' all the winners within about 5 minutes of each other.

There was one name missing from the entry list, Jimmy Guthrie who had been fatally injured in the previous year's German Grand Prix. As a tribute to this outstanding sportsman, the North of Ireland Club renamed the trophy for the Senior race. It had been presented by the City of Londonderry, he had won it on four successive years, now The Guthrie Memorial Trophy and a specially designed lid carrying a memorial inscription was added to the cup.

The North West 200 was run in very wet conditions and from the fall of the starter's flag Freddie Frith (Norton) swept into the lead, followed by Stanley (Velocette) who, feeling unwell, had been examined by a doctor just before the start. By Millburn Corner, he was only 200 yards behind with Jack Moore (Norton) and new comer Ernie Lyons (Triumph) 3rd and 4th respectively.

On the second lap Frith led Stanley by 26 seconds at Shell Bridge but on a difficult corner on the section between Portrush and Portstewart, Frith misjudged it, unhurt in the spill and was able to continue to the pits. Stanley then took the lead, challenged by Moore, who also skidded, came down but was also able to continue. After his pit stop Stanley managed to take the lead again and after thirteen laps had a 25 second advantage. On the next lap it was 47 seconds and as he flashed over the line to begin his last lap he was 65 seconds ahead with the crowd waiting to cheer the smiling Irishman, who

had not won the race since 1933. It was not to be, for it was Jack Moore (Norton) who rounded Primrose Hill and swept down towards Golf Course Corner to be flagged the winner.

Everyone was asking where was Stanley, until a phone call was received from him requesting that petrol be taken to him to enable him to bring the machine back. Ernie Lyons was 2nd and C D Foord (Norton) 3rd. Sadly, three weeks later Jack Moore from the North of England crashed on the Mountain Mile in the Isle of Man and was killed instantly.

JUNIOR TT

It was not until 1938 that Veloce Ltd achieved what they had longed for, a win in the Junior TT, which was their first since 1929. The engines were of square-finned type with single-overhead camshaft and two rockers mounted on eccentric spindles which had been introduced the previous year. The very large cylinder-head (10" square), was designed to enclose the hairpin-type valve springs and also extended into the machine's slipstream for the benefit of cooling.

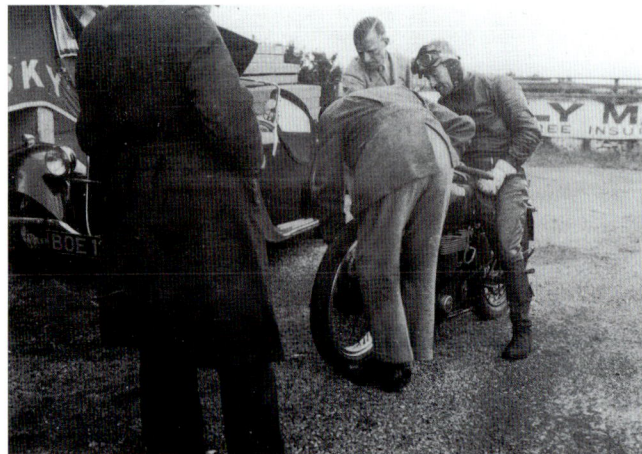

Practice period at Creg-na-Baa

Stanley, their star rider, led throughout to win from team mate Ted Mellors by four minutes, with a new lap record of 85.30 mph, so ending a seven year run of Junior wins by Norton. It was quite a performance from a single-overhead camshaft engine. The winning Velocettes were virtually indistinguishable from the previous year except for larger inlet valves, fitted just before the TT. The Velocette policy of 'racing what they sold' and improving the breed by racing was beginning to pay-off. Freddie Frith was the first Norton home, helping to regain the manufacturer's team prize.

The Nortons' were quite new with DOHC engines with extensive use of light alloy and fitted with the 'new flanged' telescopic forks, Craig had been impressed by

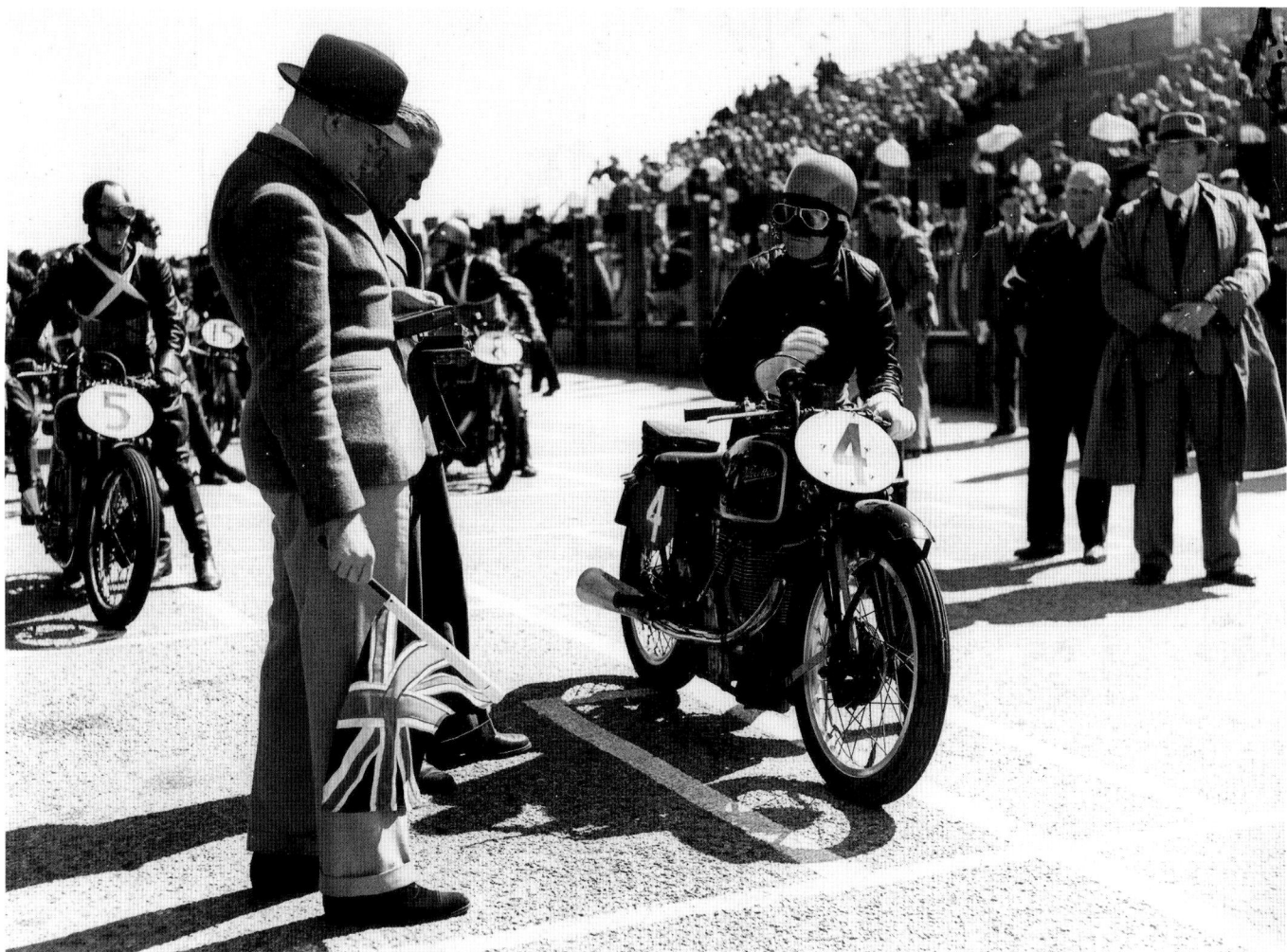

Start of the 1938 Junior TT

Stanley, Junior Velocette, Quarterbridge

the speed of the abortive DOHC Velocette of 1936 and sought to develop one and had also been impressed with the telescopic forks on the 1937 BMW which Jock West rode into sixth place. The Norton forks improved road-holding and particularly front-wheel braking. By now the true value of revolution counters were well realised.

SENIOR TT

The Norton Team of Frith, White and Daniell (who now replaced Guthrie as a full member of the team) were favourites to win the Senior TT. Once again Stanley and his 500 Velocette were the main opposition and the only man who could upset Joe Craig's plans. Frith, (the previous years winner) riding No1 set the pace for the opening laps closely followed by Stanley. An ultra quick fill-up, before going into the fourth lap put him ahead by

Riding back to winners enclosure

Governor congratulates Stanley after his 9th TT Win

Harold Willis doing his final check of Senior machine

Returning to Velocette HQ, practise day, Stanley's Delage in background

a few seconds, through laps four and five the order was Stanley, Frith and Daniell, then at Sulby on the fifth lap, signals showed Daniell coming up to challenge Frith for 2nd place.

Harold's sixth lap signal at Ramsey was a large W with 5 underneath, a colossal effort on his part put him in the lead going into the last lap by 5 seconds and posted the first ever 'under 25 minute lap' (24mins 57 secs).

Frith finished with his fastest lap of the race, just a few seconds outside of his previous record. Stanley made a desperate over-90mph last effort that pipped Frith by just 2 seconds and he narrowly missed the double.

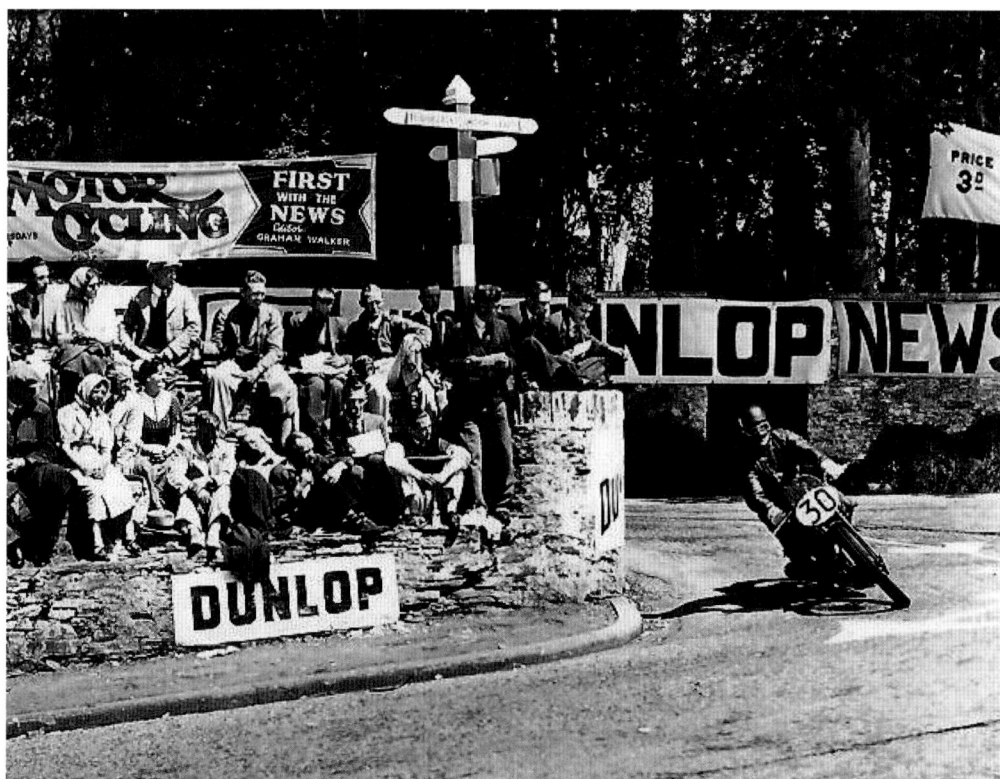

Stanley at climax of 1938 Senior

Harold Daniell, then on his last lap, raised the bar yet again to win with a record final lap of 24 mins 52 seconds, (91 mph). Stanley was very tired but happy that he had once again succeeded in splitting the opposition, but a win in that class was never to be for Velocette. White came fourth to give Norton yet another team prize.

STANLEY'S WORDS
BELGIUM GP 26TH JUNE

On the Monday morning after TT I was off on a six week racing tour with Jimmy Little. My Junior, Senior Velocettes and his KTT were on the trailer behind my Delage which was shipped at 6p.m. so I indulged in a final rush home for tea and back to docks. Hoped schedule was on time 'I always liked the back of a journey broken by lunch time'. Jimmy travelled to boat by train from Belfast. I spent time before bed writing an article, an inside story of breaking Norton's stranglehold of Junior TT and continued before breakfast. We were delayed ½ hr by crane breaking down so hoped to make up time but 30 mph on vehicles with trailers, spent afternoon at Veloce works left for London 7pm.

Booked into rooms on way, look on girls face when asked for 5am call with tea for 5.30am, on the road by six. Shortly after 9am collected our carnets from AA London

Harold Daniel during his record winning lap of 91mph

after a few calls each arrived Dover, wrote article once aboard, and posted it in Ostend with relief. Late evening headed for Bruges and again arranged an early morning call; Jimmy was getting used to this and beat me to continental coffee and rolls at 6.30a.m. On the road again, goal Brussels, then Louvain, Huy, Ardennes to Francorchamps for Belgium GP. Francorchamps is a small village 5/6 miles south of Spa with a charm and distinction all its own but cooler, most racing lads stay in Spa, several hundred feet lower and reminiscent of a Turkish Bath.

I had missed the Belgium GP for 5 years but returned to a warm welcome to the same hotel I had stayed in during my 8 years with Norton. Lunch quick check of machines before practice started at 6.30 with a couple of laps first by car to note only alterations during my absence to give Jimmy an idea where he could be going.

Once on the line I had warned Jimmy that some of the farmers never seemed to realise that the roads had been closed, I had a fright some years previous so we were in no hurry to start. By the time I had completed a couple of laps it was raining heavily so pulled in for the evening. No faults revealed so lazed in sun until lunchtime with the Norton team.

Next day lively craic with Freddy Frith and Jock West announced they were walking the course in the afternoon, 11 miles in scorching sun. We could not see the sense in walking when we had the car, we parked and walked around various bends and corners, I showed Jimmy the correct approach and therefore cut down the number of laps he would need to learn the course. I found one of the finest ways to improve my speed on a particular corner – was to get off the bike and walk giving you an entirely new idea when surveyed in this manner.

Walter Rusk and Jimmy Little

Belgium GP, Stanley leads Harold Daniel

We did this several times until Jimmy had memorised the bends etc fairly well and did not catch up with Frith / West until ¾ way round which showed what time we had spent on each corner. They refused a lift from us even though the strong sun was melting the road tar (this could cause trouble for the race if this weather did not cool).

Perfect evening for practice, couple of laps, pulled in to check plug, changed a bigger jet, another lap increase size again, another couple of laps at full throttle, no sign of heat in plug so left alone. Bike going well but troublesome flies, heat melting tar thought the roads could be in a dangerous condition.

Saturday practice from noon to 1pm, cruised around, road gang were spreading sand on melted tar making conditions even more dangerous, officials said all loose sand would be swept away before races. Official scrutineering 3.30pm, fitted number made from toughest sheet metal, a specialty of Belgium GP club. Their weight made for debate in dropping ones gear a little. Remainder of day spent swimming with Jock West, another short walk after dinner and bed. Tomorrow was another day. Race run under perfect conditions, delayed about 1 hr for road to be properly swept.

The 500 Velocette was slower than the BMW and Norton, Georg Meier (BMW) took the lead from Frith (Norton) while West, Daniell and I battled for third place, finally after 3 or 4 laps I wore them down and got away. After another lap or so I caught Frith who was obviously not flat out, I passed him and he re-passed me on the next straight and I assumed that that he was not prepared to chase Meier on the BMW, he must be aware of some weakness in his engine and perhaps trying to save it.

I believed the Velocette to be unbreakable and decided to hurry him, then on the next set of bends a rider of a 175 machine got between us and in avoiding him I got into some loose sand and gravel in the gutter (at well over 100mph) coming into a left hand 90mph bend, I lost my braking and ran off the road, crashed heavily, smashing up my left hand and lost a finger I felt that I got off very lucky, that was the end of the 1938 season".

Assisted from the crash by Belgium police

Stanley did something which he admitted later he should not have done, in passing on the outside of a fast bend, for the other rider, a Belgian, riding in the 175 class (running concurrently with the 500's) had no idea that he was approaching and strayed across his path.

JOCK WEST ON BELGIUM G.P.

"Although roughly triangular in the traditional continental manner the Spa Circuit, the home of the Belgium Grand Prix is also twists and turns for most of the length and consequently justifiably enables the more skilled competent riders to display their superiority However on arrival for the Belgium Grand Prix the competitors were badly shaken to find that the road authorities, with the best of intentions, had resurfaced most of the circuit, However they had not anticipated a heat wave of much above average temperatures which reduced the newly laid surface to a sea of molten tar. Having convinced the big wigs that the molten surface rendered racing impossible an army of workers descended on the circuit and in a remarkably short time covered the liquid surface with at least 3" of dusty top dressing. This resulted in further protests and so an army of workers were provided with large brushes and proceeded to clean a relatively narrow track along the centre of the road. Although far from perfect all agreed that the race could take place as planned.

From the start the track descended a relatively steep slope turning left and then right over a bridge before starting the steep winding mountain road. Restricted to the narrow brushed centre of the road the riders tended to bunch except a few who had made a fast start from the

Arriving at Baldonnell airport, South-west of Dublin

front of the grid. Georg Meier and Freddy Frith were two of the few who were able to choose a reasonable path drew well ahead of the pack.

At the top of the hill there is a relatively sharp left turn which caused the pack to become even more bunched, that is all except one! Unable to get past the main bunch Stanley Woods bravely took to the loose side surface and in a series of slides and wobbles made his way to the front in a valiant effort to catch up with Meier and Frith.

The main pack continued as a bunch along the second leg of the circuit but by two thirds of the way up the third and fastest leg I had managed to pull clear of the pack. On rounding a comparatively tight left hand bend I was confronted by a fallen competitor who was trying hard to pull his machine off the road and so eliminate quite a dangerous disruption to following riders.

I recognised that it was Stanley Woods and also noticed that he was only able to use one hand and was holding the other hand and arm as if it was injured.

After the race, which was won by Georg Meier with Freddie Frith second and myself third, I was asked as I was returning to the U.K. the next day if I would do my best to look after Stanley. He was most anxious to return to Dublin to receive the expert attention of a surgeon in whom he had great confidence.

I therefore called at the Spa Infirmary the following morning; I was ushered into a surgery where Stanley was receiving final attention for the journey home. The surgeon was holding and bandaging what looked very much like a beetroot but which I soon realised was Stanley's damaged hand. When handing Stanley over to my care the surgeon gave me a small glass container, which I assumed contained medicine. On looking at it carefully I saw that it was not medicine but Stanley's amputated finger, which were being returned to prove the necessity of removal.

The journey from Spa to Brussels was by train where at the airport we boarded a Sabena aircraft for London. Having had nothing to eat since an early breakfast and in the absence of time for refreshments at the airport I bought a slab of strong Belgium chocolate to sustain us until we reached Croydon. Alas! This was not a wise move as it was a most unpleasantly bumpy journey and it wasn't long before, in company with most of the passengers, I had to call for a brown bag. Meanwhile my badly injured companion, that I was supposed to be looking after, showed not a sign of sickness

At Croydon, the Mobil Oil representative, Bert Perkins, met us and after a short wait at the airport hotel we saw Stanley off on his own to his good and capable medical friends in Dublin, complete with his glass jar and his finger preserved in surgical spirit".

EARLS COURT MOTORCYCLE SHOW 1938

With huge crowds it was almost impossible to get anywhere near the Velocette stand at Earls Court, where the star of the show was the last and most famous of the KTT Racers - the Mark V111 - a production version of the works development model on which Stanley had broken Norton's dominance of the Junior TT only a few months earlier.

As well as riding, Stanley had worked on the development side, for he had a gift to sense faults and an ability to make suggestions to correct them. When Veloce eventually produced a class winning machine, one of the conditions not

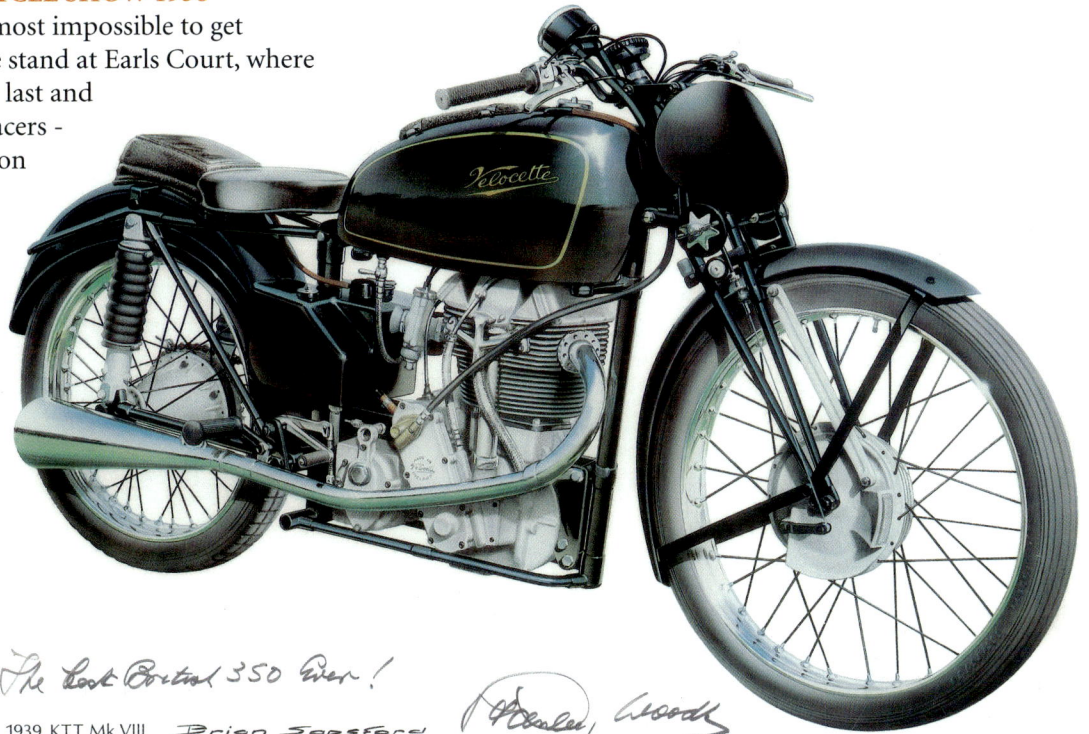

The Last Bristol 350 Ever !

1939 KTT Mk VIII *Brian Sepsford*

Stanley Woods

May 1939 Australian Frank Mussett and New Zealander Len Parry collect their MKV111 Velocettes at Hall Green en route to TT

written into his agreement was that they would produce 'As near as possible' a replica and not a 'look a like'.

It was built in limited numbers for selected riders before the outbreak of war in 1939. Each engine was bench tested to a specific power, and not released until that figure was passed. Stanley always regarded himself as largely responsible for the development of the rolling chassis of a machine which was virtually a 'Works' bike as used between 1936 and 1938.

1939
LEINSTER 200 13th May
The Leinster 200 held at Tallagh Co Dublin was titled The Grand Prix of Eire and marked the return of Stanley to racing after the injury to his left

Tallagh Start

Only time a motorcycle GP was held in Eire

Stanley in pit with Jimmy Little (centre)

Stanley way out in front

hand the previous June. Those who had any doubts about his ability to handle racing machines soon had them dispelled. That year riding a 'Pukka' model, despite a poor start and melting tar in places due to the hot sun, he was in great form and rode with all his dash winning the 350cc class and putting in a lap of 84.52mph, the fastest lap ever accomplished on the circuit including cars.

North West 200

The road racing season in Northern Ireland opened with the North West 200. This was the debut of the liquid-cooled four-cylinder AJS entered by Associated Motorcycles Ltd and provided an exciting treat for the spectators. From the start Stanley established a comfortable lead and left the rest of the field headed by Ernie Lyons (Triumph) and Bill Beevers (Norton) far behind.

May, Portstewart, Co Londonderry, Jimmy Little Velocette takes the flag to win the 350 Class of the North West 200

Stanley always meticulous about his preparations

Ernie Lyons (Triumph) the eventual winner

Foster eventually got the 'Blown Four' going well and ploughed his way through the 250's, but going through the 350's he locked handlebars with another rider who crashed fortunately unhurt.

Stanley increased his lead and set up the fastest lap of the day but on his third circuit he went out with a seized engine.

After refuelling, Foster retired on the 13th lap with a blown cylinder head gasket and Lyons took the flag at reduced speed, when rain fell during the closing laps.

TT

Most people felt that it might be the last of the series for some considerable time but despite being run in an uneasy atmosphere, the entries were well up on previous years. Stanley had felt a little unwell off and on since the previous spring and had decided not to book into a hotel as he needed a special milk food diet, so they rented a private house near the start and finish area.

Mildred's younger sister Nora had come with them and it was not long before they were joined by Len Perry a well known New Zealand rider whom they had known for some time. He had to have a finger amputated following his crash on the Mark V111 Velocette in first practice just before Ballacraine. While recovering they offered him a place to stay for the remainder of the TT period, the foursome got on well and was reported to have had a right good time together.

Stanley's retainer had been cut by 25% according to Veloce Ltd to help to pay for the development of the new experimental twin that Harold Willis had been working on over the winter. According to Stanley it was for not

I rode this machine for one lap in T.T. practice, just to show that we were trying – Its potential was terrific but the war put a stop to all that! Stanley Woods

completing his full year's contract as a result of his accident the previous June in the Belgium Grand Prix.

He had already made up his mind that he would not ride the 500 Single if he were to sign up for them for the 1940 season as he felt it had become a little uncompetitive as it was an older design the engine should have been upgraded to Double Overhead Camshaft.

However, for the 1939 TT Charles Udall and mechanic Tommy Mutton arrived on the Island on 8th June with the new machine, a complete departure from anything seen before - a Supercharged Vertical Twin, affectionately known as the 'Roarer', with two contra-rotating crankshafts geared together revolving in line with the frame in opposite directions to achieve a near perfect balance. Its clutch and four speed gearbox were housed within large oval crankcases and driven from the left side crankshaft. The supercharger mounted on the side of the gearbox was driven by the right-side crankshaft; final drive was by shaft and bevel to the rear hub. The frame constructed mostly of tubes and welded was thought to be the first of its kind. It also used full width alloy hubs on both wheels.

At first Velocette wanted to use tele-forks but with an anticipated speed of 145mph at 7000rpm Stanley insisted on Webb forks which had been used successfully on the singles.

Velocette HQ (left to right) Charles Udall, Stanley and race mechanic with Junior machine

Moto Guzzi HQ) Stanley (centre) O Tenni and Giorgio Parodi

That evening Stanley was able to take it out of the Nursery Hotel in Onchan (Velocette headquarters) and up the slip road to Signpost Corner for a run over the course, reporting that it was the best steering motorcycle that he had ever ridden. Teething troubles with the Supercharger prevented its use in the Senior Race and the stable relied on the faithful single.

After a hectic practice period, on the last Saturday morning before the race Stanley left the Nursery Hotel to give the 350 a final practice. The machine was the same as in 1937 but had undergone modifications to the

Parodi (Moto Guzzi owner) Tenni with 250 racer and Stanley's personal transport KSS Velocette

inlet valve tract and for the TT was fitted with a special low bottom gear, which was known to give some advantage in parts of the course such as Ramsey Hairpin, The Gooseneck, etc. when he reached Kirk Michael he saw there were signs of a fall by the wayside, for Ginger Wood had crashed and entered someone's garden, so he decided to save all the fireworks for Monday.

Happy with the machine but a little doubtful about the accuracy of the rev counter, a new one was fitted before the bike was handed over to the scrutineers.

The next day, the eve of the Junior TT, the death of Harold Willis was announced at a hospital in Birmingham. A respected and very likeable person had gone and everyone felt a sense of personal loss. He had been ill with meningitis and died from complications that followed a relatively minor operation. Harold a director of Veloce Limited, a self-taught engineer was intimately connected with the development and preparation of the race machines. He was 39 years of age and had competed in a number of Tourist Trophy races, placing second twice on Velocettes in the 1927 and 1928 Junior races. His role was taken on by his assistant Charles Udall.

JUNIOR TT

On race day as the starting time drew near Stanley felt a bit nervy, but confident of being able to win.

The 1939 Junior TT has been described as a 'Thrilling Triangular' contest, a furious battle between Velocette, Norton and DKW, where the previous recorded speed would never be attained owing to the strong bitter wind. Freddie Frith (Norton) led Stanley Woods (Velocette) by a small margin for the first three laps until the Norton began to loose power and stopped on the fourth lap. Daniell who had taken a toss at Ramsey remounted and began to close on Stanley with Fleischmann DKW lagging in 3rd place.

Stanley later said it had been one of the hardest races of his career his chin had been on the tank for most of the time, his damaged left hand holding on with only three fingers with his

Stanley warms up Velocette before the start of the Junior Race

thumb propped up on top of the handlebar – the hand needed a massage when he finished. He also said he had ridden according to plan but that on the last lap Daniell had rather caught him napping meaning he had won by the narrow margin of eight seconds. Velocette gained the team prize.

At the prize distribution in the Villa Marina that evening Stanley received a wonderful ovation, this win had formed a personal triumph without parallel in the history of the Tourist Trophy for it had raised his total number of successes to double figures (10 in all) four Seniors, five Juniors and a Lightweight.

Stanley Junior Velocette Bray Hill

Stanley through Quarterbridge

LIGHTWEIGHT TT

The decision by Moto Guzzi to send two supercharged singles plus mechanics to the Isle of Man for Omobono Tenni and Stanley, plus entries from DKW and Benelli concentrated a lot of interest in the Lightweight event. The race was held in wet and miserable conditions and by the end of the first lap Tenni led Stanley by 8 seconds, with Ted Mellors (Benelli) 37 seconds behind in 3rd place. On lap 2 Stanley had a long stop with ignition problems which left him in eighth place, while Tenni was now slowing. Mellors then took the lead with Ewald Kluge (DKW) moving into third spot and from then he never looked back, going on to victory. Tenni retired at Ballaugh on lap 3.

At the end of lap 4 Stanley moved up to 3rd behind Mellors and Kluge having just made the fastest lap of the race at 78.16 mph, despite worsening rain and decreasing visibility on the mountain, but his race ended at Crosby on lap 5 with a dead engine.

Although he had won many important Continental races, it had long been Ted Mellor's ambition to win a TT.

SENIOR TT

Although none of his friends and admirers knew it, this was to be Stanley's last ever TT.

The supercharged BMW's had contested the TT in both 1937 and 1938 without success. Now lighter (304lbs) with improved steering and a power output of 68 b.h.p., this was around 20 more than a British single and no one could touch them. Tragedy had struck the BMW team when Austrian Karl Gall died in Ramsey Cottage hospital after a practice crash at Ballaugh, leaving Georg Meier and Jock West to ride the flat-twins.

Georg Meier started No. 49 and from there dominated the Senior. Stanley & Jock West tied initially for second place but gradually the two BMWs that Stanley reckoned were "15 miles an hour faster", pulled away from the Velocette. He had a disastrous pit stop at the end of the third lap when it took three tries to get the bike to re-start and was now down to fourth place behind Frith.

Whilst Stanley got ahead again well into the third, Freddie regained the position on the last lap by just 2 seconds. Velocette won the Manufacturers Prize and the

Two young girls watch as Stanley passes hedge of No 2 Signalling Station on his way to winning his Tenth Tourist Trophy

Harold Daniel (Norton) 2nd, Heiner Fleiscmann (DKW) 3rd, congratulate Stanley

Stanley's Senior Velocette at Keppel Gate

trio of Woods (4th) Mellors (7th) & Whitworth (12th) won the club prize for the Derby M.C.C.

ULSTER GRAND PRIX

In late spring the Ulster Motor Cycle Club had taken the decision to abandon the Ulster Grand Prix on account of the demands made by the government of Northern Ireland as regards insurance for the meeting. Finally they rescinded their demand and offered to allow the club to organise the race with the same insurance as was affected the previous years.

BMW did not contest the Ulster Grand Prix as most of their riders were unfit following crashes in Sweden and Germany.

Having won the 'Ulster' Senior event for them in 1937 and '38 on the ultra-fast Clady circuit and confident of a 'Hat trick', Jock West and his wife, as part of their honeymoon, travelled to Germany and pleaded with the company for a machine, but to no avail. With the outbreak of the war looming they were quite firm about this. Instead they lent them a car for a week-long tour of Austria.

On their return they were taken to the airport and that was the last that Jock would see of BMW until after the war.

Jock West on practise day riding Georg Meier's BMW No 49 while his own was being repaired. Returning after Karl Gall's fatal crash with his helmet strapped to his belt.

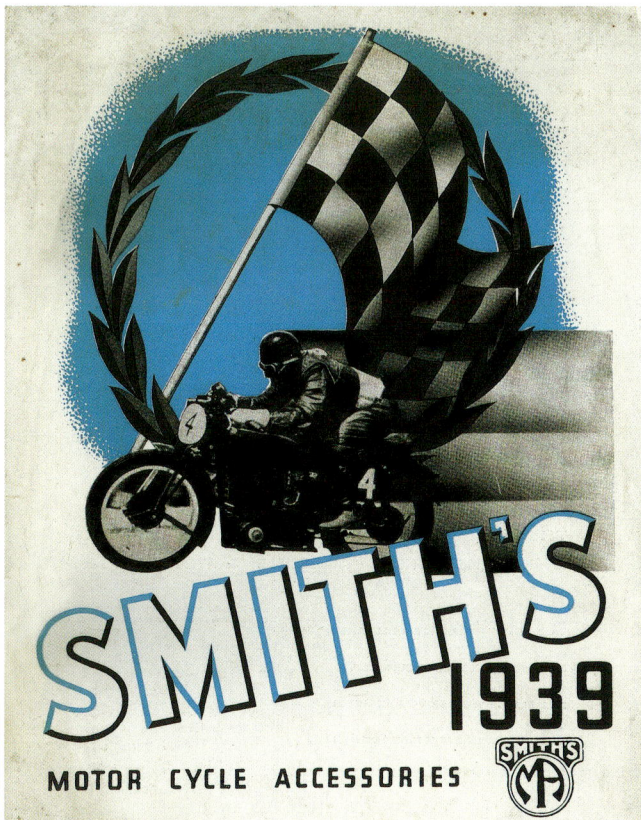

SMITH'S 1939
MOTOR CYCLE ACCESSORIES

Practise day. Matt Wright makes adjustments to Walter Rusk's Blown (V4 AJS)

Walter Rusk (V4 AJS)

Dorino Serafini (Supercharged 4 Cylinder Gilera)

Junior winner Stanley Woods in his last ever road race

Dorino Serafini won the 500cc Class at a record average speed of 97.85mph, the tremendous power and speed of the supercharged four cylinder Gilera easily beat Freddie Frith's brave attempts on the 'unblown' Works Norton. It was in this race that Walter Rusk (V4-AJS) did the first ever lap at 100mph on a British Road Circuit, before retiring on the fourth lap with a broken lower fork link. Serafini then upped the record to

100.03mph and also clinched the European 500cc Championship.

This was the last ever Motor Grand Prix to be won by a machine with forced induction (Supercharging).

With the different classes to run concurrently, Stanley decided to contest the 'Ulster' on his 350cc Velocette. Interest in the class was keen by the entry of two German DKW's ridden by Siegfried Wuensche and

Dublin University MCC 1939 Fall Trial

Heiner Fleschmann who had finished the Junior TT in third place behind Stanley and Ted Mellors, so another three-way tussle was expected. Eventually, after a cat and mouse game with team mate Ted Mellors, Stanley won at an average of 96.65 mph.

CAR RACING

Because of his motorcycling commitments Stanley only drove occasionally. In 1939 he entered The Leinster Trophy at Tallaght in July, The Ballinascorney Hill Climb in August, (retired in both) and the IMRC Phoenix Park in September, driving a Morgan and finishing 5th. He found car racing most enjoyable though some of the other drivers resented the fact that he got most of the publicity. An able and enthusiastic driver, he never had the best of cars. Although he got well paid, he was a great motorcyclist who failed to make the transition to cars. During those last two seasons he had been experiencing some health problems; an inflammatory bowel condition which was also having an effect on his eyesight, but this was not diagnosed and treated until 1946. This left him in a dispirited mood at times, which was another little known reason why he might have had to give up racing.

CHAPTER EIGHT
1939-1945

EMERGENCY YEARS

FROM 1936 TO 1939 Stanley was living part-time in London in a rented house. Under contract with Veloce Ltd., he also had a winter job with Mobil Oil.

Upon the outbreak of war in early September, he phoned a friend with connections in the Irish defence forces saying: *"Well, you know by now that I am out of a job"*. *"What would you like to do"?* Was his reply. Stanley said *"I would like to join the army; I was a school boy cadet"*. *"Ours or theirs"* he asked. *"Ours if they will have me"* continued Stanley. *"Leave it with me"* said his friend.

Stanley put his affairs in order and entered the Irish Defence Forces as a 2nd Lieutenant in the Volunteer Force (this was the reserve component), on 24th October 1939 and reported for permanent service on 27th October 1939.

One day a short time later, he found himself in front of the 'Top brass' and was questioned. *"Lieutenant Woods, we would like your opinion as we are thinking of purchasing Royal Enfield motorcycles for the defence forces"*. *"Sorry Sir"* was his reply, *"As a shareholder in that company I could not possibly give my opinion"*.

The officer said *"Never mind that we would like your opinion anyway"*. *"Don't"* Stanley replied.

His advice was ignored by the Army and they went ahead, purchasing the first batch.

The Irish Army had imported a trial order of three Belgium Gillet motorcycles in the 1930s. Unfortunately these were 500cc OHV Sports machines and were quite unsuitable for army service.

Captain Woods giving instruction

Stanley and Mildred (Ex Works BSA 350)

Stanley served with the Supply & Transport Corps for the duration of his service and held the appointment of Officer-in-charge of the Motorcycle Section at the base workshops in Clancy Barracks, Islandbridge, Dublin. He trained motorcyclists for military operations and display purposes, teaching them the art of riding in all terrain and weather conditions, especially how to fall off safely. Most of the men did not like the latter, but after the war many of them became very successful competition riders.

During WW1 various armies found motorcycles indispensable and again they were to have an important role to play in WWII.

He insisted in the promotion of trials and cross country riding as an essential part of military training. They certainly had an expert teacher, for he was a man of

Stanley films Mildred holding niece Heather Burney after her christening Mountmerrion July 1941

The Tenth Annual
Dublin "100"
Handicap road race for solo motor cycles
incorporating
The National 100 Miles Championships of Ireland

AT THE PHŒNIX PARK, DUBLIN

SATURDAY, 6th JULY, 1940
AT 3.30 P.M.
Dublin and District Motor Cycle Club, Limited

["*Irish Independent*" Photo]

Dublin 100 programme with inserted photo of Stanley in 1939 Leinster 200 but as he was a serving Army officer he did not compete

1942 Ernie Lyons, Stanley Woods, P. Sargent, W. Leonard at Lamb's Doyle, Dublin - Manders Cup Trial

considerable reputation as an off-road rider, having an unprecedented five wins in Ireland's premier trial The Patland cup and in many other competitions.

One day during a training exercise, a soldier seemed for no apparent reason to loose control of his machine. He was about to be put on a charge when Lieutenant Woods intervened, requesting the machine to be brought to the workshops. There he had the steering stripped out and the mechanics found cracked bearings. Stanley was not surprised, even though this was quite a new model. Acting on his advice the army decided to strip down the steering heads of every third machine and what they found resulted in the whole batch being sent back to England and replaced with the time trusted BSA M20.

Around this time Stanley wrote to his old friend Bert Perrigo, the competition manager at Birmingham Small

Falling off BSA M20

Arms (BSA) inquiring if there were a genuine trials machine lying in some corner of the works that might be for disposal. The result was that he was given a nearly new 1939 350cc OHV ex factory machine; he was actually charged £5 for the model in case of injury or even worse so his next of kin could not claim from the company. Stanley took this machine out occasionally and gave his Sergeant instructors a run on it to see what a real machine was like across country.

In January 1940 Stanley was promoted to Lieutenant and by October promoted again to Captain. He was a competent officer and confessed that he was shocked at the state of the army in the early days of the 'Emergency', as it was called. Eire's defence force had seen a rapid rate of expansion though pay remained low.

There was a real fear of the likelihood of a German invasion in 1940 as a part of a larger strategy for attacking Britain and there were all kinds of censorship of press, radio and mail.

In 1942 with some of his assets tied up in England he decided to come clean with the Revenue Commissioners in Dublin and had to pay them a four figure sum. Mildred's parents had long returned to their native Belfast and as a serving Officer in the Irish Army, he had to apply for permission to travel to Northern Ireland. It was during one of these trips that he recorded a 15 minute programme. It was as part of a series for the BBC Radio entitled 'Giants of Sport', due to be broadcast in July 1942.

'GIANTS OF SPORT' INTERVIEW

The final question the compere asked him was *"Which race of all your races did you enjoy most"*. He replied *"Without question the last one The 1939 Ulster Grand Prix. From the very beginning it was a terrific struggle you see my machine was not the fastest one in the race; and any lack of speed in a fast race like the Ulster is an almost unbeatable handicap but tactics gave me the lead at half distance and enabled me to hold it to the finish."*
Compere: *"Well let's finish up with the story."*
Stanley *"It's rather a long story but I'll make it as short as I can. I was riding in the 350 Class on a Velocette and during the race I discovered what I had suspected earlier that my team mate Ted Mellors was on a mount which was pulling a higher gear than mine. I used everything I had but we both realised that he had that little extra which was going to make all the difference so I had to pull a bit of a stunt. The race was over 11 laps and before the start we had arranged that I would stop to refuel after 5 laps and Mellors after 6. I knew that my pit work would be really snappy and I banked everything on it. I let Ted increase his lead slightly lap after lap until nearly the end of the 5th then I got a little nearer but not near enough to let him feel that there was any danger then once round Clady Corner I gave her all she had I was right on his heels when I came into the pits for just about the quickest fill up I ever had. Everything worked out just as I had hoped it would, I got away for a really hot lap, took every corner and bend as fast as I knew how and when I got round to the pits again there was Ted still astride his bike. Well! It meant that I had a few seconds at worst plus the difference between my flying start at maximum speed and his push start, it was enough, one more hectic lap and I was signalled that I could afford to ease off a little. Poor Mellors didn't even get 2nd place though, he crashed on his*

Mildred with Stanley and other Officers. Second from left is Captain Harold Rae, a well known 1930s Irish trials rider

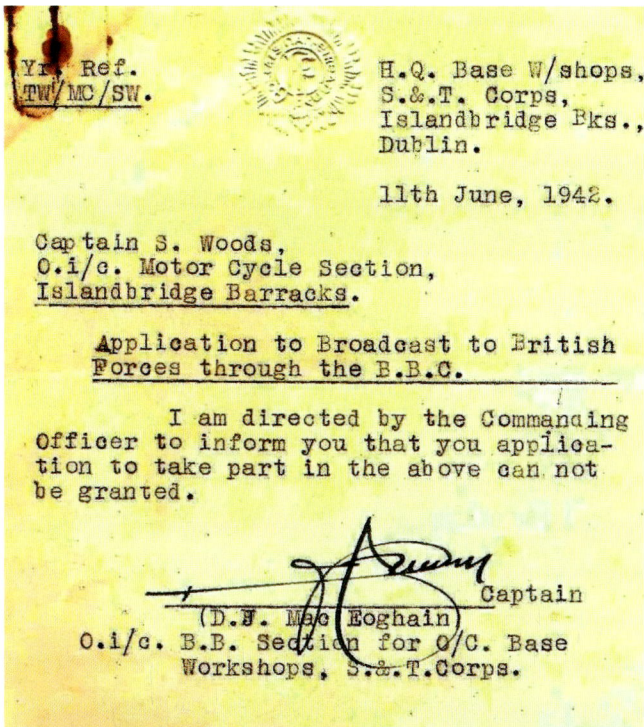

last lap damaged his machine and was forced to retire... Yes, I really do think that was the most enjoyable race in my whole career"

Compere: "It seems a rather distant prospect at the moment but I think we all hope that you will have many more big races and more Laurels too. Well thank you very much."

Stanley was promoted to Commandant in January 1943 (the equivalent in the British Army's rank of Major).

During these years Stanley revealed yet another of his talents by writing many articles for 'The Motorcycle', as he had always been on friendly terms with the editor Arthur Bourne.

During eleven days of leave in June 1944 while writing a series of articles, which were never published, about the crashes that he had had over the years he realised how dangerous it had become.

He had witnessed his team mate Tim Hunt's terrible crash in 1933 in Sweden which ended his career along with the death of his good friend Jimmy Guthrie in 1937 at the German GP.

Stanley had a very safe riding career but by 1934 was riding as an individual not a member of a team. His own two crashes at the 1934 Dutch TT and 1938 Belgium GP in June, when he lost his left index finger, each cost him the most of a year's competition and nearly his life. He decided there and then, that after 19 years of the most

Stanley and Ernie Lyons, Curragh 1945

Commandant Stanley Woods, 1943

intensive competition he would be hanging up his crash hat for good as far as road racing was concerned and told his wife Mildred of his decision - the war had saved his life!!

Just after the war in Europe had ended, as part of a military tattoo, Stanley organised a motorcycle display at the RDS (Royal Dublin Society) show grounds. With riders jumping off ramps and some standing on saddles

RDS Showground Military Tattoo

Dear Commandant Woods,

I received your letter of the 23rd instant and wish to state that it has been arranged to promote you to the rank of Major on your last day of Permanent Service. It is regretted that it is not possible to promote you to the rank of Major earlier as it would create a precedent.

Yours sincerely,

Commandant Stanley Woods,
"The Dell",
Torquay Road,
Foxrock,
Co. Dublin.

A.F. 452(c). No. 810

ÓGLAIGH NA hÉIREANN.

CERTIFICATE OF SERVICE AS AN OFFICER.

This is to Certify that

(Rank) Major
(Name) Stanley Woods
(Corps or Service) Supply and Transport
served as a Commissioned Officer in the
~~Reserve of Officers~~
*Reserve of Officers (Volunteer Force)
from 27th October, 1939
to 19th August, 1946
6 years 45 days of which were given on Permanent Service.
Termination of service was due to Resignation.

REMARKS: Pursuant to Article 6 of Emergency Powers No.37) Order, 1940, the Minister for Defence has consented to the retention by the abovenamed of his uniform.

Signed at Department of Defence this Twentieth day of August 1946.

J. Flynn COLONEL
Adjutant General

*Strike out where inapplicable.

NOTE : No particulars further to those contained in this Form will be furnished.

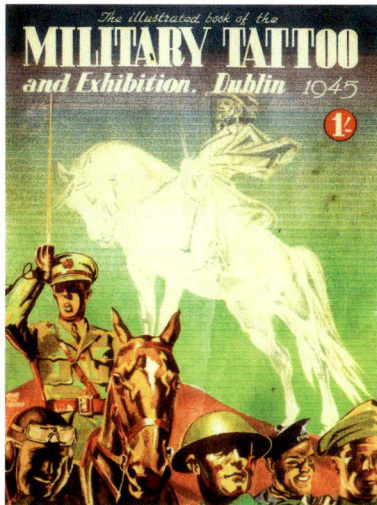

of moving bikes while drinking a pint of Guinness, this part of the show was a great success.

He wrote to the Chief of Staff to inform him that on his intended retirement from the Army in about a month's time he

Ballyednumduff Trial

This was the first trial in Eire after the war

would like the rank of Major as he had an international reputation and the rank of Commandant was not understood abroad except in France.

The reply received stated: 'the Minister was favourably disposed to promote him to the rank of Major but he would like to have the views of the military members of the Defence Council'.

He was released from permanent service at his own request, with effect from 11th December 1945 and resigned his commission on 20th August 1946.

THE BURNEY CONNECTION

John Paul Burney had been an accomplished racing cyclist and was a pioneer motorcyclist of the early 1900s. He represented the Enfield Cycle Co for Ireland and moved from Belfast to Rathmines Dublin with his family in 1907.

BURNEY BROS.,
Motor Engineers,
67, GT. BRUNSWICK STREET,
DUBLIN.

In 1920 he formed a new company with his eldest son Gordon, named Burney Bros Motor Engineers 67 Great Brunswick Street Dublin (later renamed Pearse Street) with agencies for British and American cars and Royal Enfield motorcycles.

Gordon followed in his father's footsteps into the motorcycle sport and soon became friends with an up and coming rider – Stanley Woods, who lived nearby. Gordon had great success in Irish events including a win in the 350 Class of the 1925 Ulster Grand Prix on a Royal Enfield of course and gave very good performances on the Isle of Man.

Like many other riders he could not race abroad because of his commitments to the family business. It was through that friendship that Gordon first met Stanley's sister Violet and they married in the Unitarian Church St. Stephens Green Dublin in July 1930. Their only child Heather was born in June 1941.

With his younger son Desmond in 1938 another company was registered for the manufacture of Enfield bicycles - J. P. Burney & Son, cycle and oil dealers 53/54 Sandwith Street just round the corner from their main showroom.

John Paul Burney died in 1949, Violet in 1978 and Gordon in 1982.

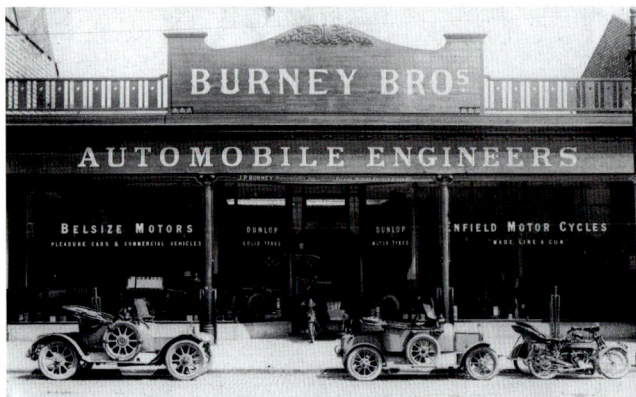

Burney Brothers, 1920

Burney Brothers garage in 1938

Gordon and his Father J.P. Burney in 1930s

CHAPTER NINE
1946-1969

1946

IN THE SPRING of 1946 Stanley entered the Motor Trade in partnership with his brother-in-law Gordon Burney, registered as Stanley Woods and Burney at the old Burney Bros. premises 67 Pearse St. Dublin.

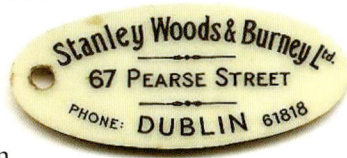

At first they bought up many second hand pre-war cars as they could get, they had already the agency for Morris/ Riley and were soon appointed all Ireland agents for Daimler.

It was in a Daimler that Stanley and Mildred travel to Kanderstay, Switzerland in February for a skiing holiday.

On crossing the Channel from Dover they witnessed the devastation from the war all along the French coast.

Stanley with new BSA Trials machine first registered to Birmingham Small Arms in January 1946

It had also been arranged for them to pay a visit to his old friend Giorgio Parodi, the Moto Guzzi boss. During the war the factory had been turned over to military production, now already thinking of the future and the new motorcycles which would be built. Now that peace had returned they were anxious to return to racing but were very short of money as the Parodi's had lost most of their shipping line in the war.

The Daimler at home, Spring 1947

Stanley agreed to sponsor two riders of his choice and Parodi would send two racers, a 250 single and a 500 wide-angle twin to the Island for the 1947 TT, plus a 500 Dondolino.

Giorgio, who came over for race week reckoned that the latter was unbreakable and should be used by the riders for practice. Stanley had previously been asked to bring out as many racing spark-plugs as he could find, as they were unobtainable at that time in Italy. He asked Manliff Barrington to ride the 250, having already signed up Freddie Frith for the 500.

Barrington was a 32 year old Dublin rider with a good pre-war record whose first shot at racing was the 1932 Cookstown 100, he said *"Stanley Woods had inspired him more than anyone else, his easy style made it look so simple as was his utterly professional approach to racing"*.

1946 Hurst Trial

Freddie Frith returned to the Island in 1947, entered on a Velocette in the Junior and the Guzzi Twin for the Senior. On the very first practice lap he crashed at Ballacraine when the front brake of the Guzzi grabbed and he suffered a broken collar-bone.

This incident caused quite a bit of panic as most of the leading riders had had their brakes relined by Ferodo since arriving on the Island. So all had their wheels stripped out, checked and proved to be correct.

With no other suitable replacement rider around Stanley was sorely tempted to take over the ride. His decision to quit racing at the outbreak of war had been an easy one, but sticking to it was quite another. He remembered the promise that he had made to his wife and scratched the entry, whilst thinking that he could easily have won.

Manliff Barrington on Bray Hill

As for the Lightweight 250 race, Manliff was fastest in practice. Maurice Cann, the main opposition, turned up on the Island with a glistening 250 Moto Guzzi that he had purchased from the works, starting No 3 and setting off at a scorching pace.

Stanley congratulating Barrington, Guzzi mechanic Agostini wearing beret

By the end of the first lap he led Manliff by 10 secs; Les Archer's (New Imperial) was 3rd 1 min 52 secs behind. The end of the second lap and the lead was cut to 7 secs, throughout the third lap Cann maintained a slender lead with Archer's pre-war machine, now 3 mins behind. In lap four Manliff had eased off a little and was trailing by 46 secs.

Then on lap six on the scoreboard, Manliff was shown to have a 2 sec lead, even though his lap time was only 0.09 mph faster than Cann, was there a timing error? We will never know!

Manliff held his lead and took the chequered flag and Maurice lodged a protest in the paddock afterwards, which was turned down and Manliff was declared the winner. Manliff and Stanley both agreed that there was probably a timing error.

1947

Maurice Cann got his revenge at the Ulster Grand Prix when after 6 hectic laps between Barrington and himself,

Benjy Russell (250 Moto Guzzi) with Stanley before the start of Lightweight MGP

Barrington's megaphone came loose and on the 7th lap came off altogether and he had to settle for 2nd place.

It was on that same Moto Guzzi that Ben B Russell a protégé of Stanley Woods was entered in the Lightweight Manx GP. Benjy (as he was better known) from Kilternan Co. Dublin, a 28 year old grass track rider, had his first road race in the Skerries 100 only weeks before.

Benjy, who had been fastest in practice, led after the first lap and was still leading when on the 5th lap he misjudged the left hand bend at School House Corner and was killed instantly.

Benjy Russell

A marshall Stanley had known from before the war and had taken an interest in Benjy (who was wearing Stanley's leathers and orange helmet) later told that on that fateful lap he seemed suddenly to sit up loose control, slid across the road towards the right kerb he just missed a big pole but hit his head off a small concrete post and suffered massive head injuries.

Stanley had seen death and injury during his racing career but the death of his supported rider affected him deeply.

The legendary MGP rider Austin Monks won the race on another Guzzi.

1948

The winter of 1946-47 had been the worst in living memory all over Europe with fuel supplies already low following the Second World War, but by 1948 there was an expectation that petrol would now be more plentiful, so second hand cars and motorcycles and what few new ones were available, continued to sell well.

Stanley, still a very popular figure, returned to the Island again as Moto Guzzi team manager to Manliff Barrington on the 250cc, with 1946 MGP winner Ernie Lyons and Omobono Tenni riding the 500 twins.

After an early lead Barrington and Tommy Wood (Moto Guzzi) retired, Maurice Cann (Moto Guzzi) went on to win the Lightweight from second man Ronald Pike (Rudge) by 10 minutes. Norton fortunes did not look good for the Senior with the Guzzi riders Tenni and Lyons fastest in practice. Ernie made a fast start only to run out of brakes at the Bungalow and crash on the first lap.

Just before the race, for some unknown reason, the mechanics had changed the front wheel of his machine, which proved faulty. After the crash he never received any medical attention and took the mountain railway back to Douglas – Nothing was ever mentioned of the incident.

Towards the end of TT week Stanley bought Giorgio Parodi a Manx tabby kitten

Winner, Austin Monks

Stanley with Omobono Tenni

Ernie Lyons (Guzzi 500 Twin) with Stanley and mechanics

from the 'Cattery' near the Grandstand and the team flew home along with the kitten. The next letter from Giorgio told Stanley that the kitten had died on the flight as they crossed the Alps, because the aircraft was not pressurised.

Mechanics Morretto, Bettega & Micucci and Omobono Tenni holding kitten about to board at Ronaldsway

Manliff Barrington adjusting chin strap before start

Stanley, Reg Armstrong, Manliff Barrington, Mildred and Fred Armstrong

Weeks later Omobono Tenni, Italy's best loved rider, who had finished 9th in the Senior TT, was involved in a fatal crash during practice at Berne, Switzerland.

1949

Woods & Burney were told a batch of Daimler cars were available, with prices due to increase, they were offered them at the old price if they could act quickly. Stanley made an appointment with his bank manager to have his overdraft extended but was turned down. He walked across the street to another bank where he did not hold an account and was successful. In the 1980s this particular bank's advertising slogan became 'We're the bank that likes to say yes'.

Manliff was again entered by Stanley on the Moto Guzzi single for the Lightweight TT. The race was started in lines of five and he led until he refuelled but was delayed with a broken valve spring.

Tommy Wood (Moto Guzzi) took the lead, but by the 6th lap Dickie Dale (Moto Guzzi) led by nearly two minutes. Just as he appeared a likely winner he retired with engine trouble, so Manliff won with Tommy Wood 12 seconds behind and Roland Pike (Rudge) 3rd.

For the Senior race Stanley entrusted the 500 Guzzi

to someone with a profound knowledge of the Isle of Man course, an old hand, Bob Foster, who led for most of the race until, 2 laps from the finish, his clutch cried 'enough' at Sulby.

The race was won by Harold Daniel (Norton) with a fastest lap of 89.75 mph by Bob Foster (Moto Guzzi). All of these riders were employed by Moto Guzzi for specific races and not on a full year's contract as in later years .

1949 was the first time that a young rider called Geoff Duke caught Stanley's eye. He described Geoff's riding style as "Like water pouring from a tap".

1950-1967

Ernie Callaghan was introduced to Stanley at a Phoenix Park event in 1932 as a very young man, claiming to be his biggest fan and from there on they became firm friends for the rest of their lives. Ernie became a salesman in 1945 at The Erne Motor Co. the importers of James motorcycles.

In 1949 the first 6E Villiers engined machine arrived and as his girlfriend Helen was considering buying a bike, a purchase was made at £72.10s.6d. As a member of

Stanley and Mildred with James in 1950

staff he was allowed to have the 10s 6d knocked off as discount! Having ridden it he realised it could be converted to a little trials bike for Helen, so he set too and made the necessary modifications.

On 20th February 1950 Helen made her competition debut (to much amusement) in a Clubman Trial where only beginners were allowed to compete and where there were all sorts of machines on the line.

At the announcement of results their prototype had won and after a wash down and oil she rode it into work

the next morning. She continued to use the bike for general purposes and any suitable trials at the weekends. ....

Meanwhile Ernie was improving same, making up bits and pieces and eventually riding it in the bigger events. He found it most enjoyable, particularly on cross-country, where he found he could keep up with 350 & 500 machines.

Stanley was away skiing most of this time, so only found out what was going on when they met out practising one Sunday. He seemed to pay little attention to Helen playing around on it, but the next Friday he came over with his car and trailer and enquired if he could borrow the James for the weekend.

A fortnight later he came back and asked if he could have it again, this time for a week. On returning it he asked if he could enter it in the Patland Cup Trial which was considered a great honour, except for the fact that Ernie had wanted to ride it himself.

On 1st April 1950 No 21 S Woods on the 197cc James started in the Patland Cup Trial and finished 5th overall on what was an ordinary road bike.

A few weeks' later two crated James motorcycles arrived at The Erne Motor Co., for the attention of Mr. Stanley Woods who came with his trailer once more and took them away. Always having a great eye for detail, he then carried out all the modifications on both, returning one to the company the other he retained, free of charge.

Cork Grand Trial

Stanley appeared James mounted on the front of the next James sales catalogue and for quite a few years rode James in off-road competition.

Ernie Callaghan went on to hold the high office of President of the Motorcycle Union of Ireland.

1953 SCOTT TRIAL

Stanley's first taste of Yorkshire's famous Scott Trial was when he joined Norton in 1926. In the 1953 event he managed to break a leg in an accident at 2 mph, so whilst in hospital a local competitor took charge of his James machine.

On his return to Ireland it had been arranged that the bike would be ridden to the nearest railway station for transit to Dublin.

The rider realised that it had a little bit more pep than his own similar model, so he wrote to Stanley, who replied that he had used 'National Benzole' mixture which gave the engine a little more urge and also ran cooler. During the war when petrol was unavailable in Ireland he developed a two-stroke engine to run on 'Spud Alcohol'.

After his return to business they took out an agency for Sun Motorcycles, Motor vehicles had to be imported in CKD (complete knock down) form and assembled in Ireland to avoid extra Import Duty but nothing seemed to fit or line up properly. Stanley phoned the company one day inquiring if they had jigs . They said *"Yes of course"*. Stanley replied, *"Well for God's sake would you use them?"*

1954-1957

In 1954 they were appointed Moto Guzzi Concessionaires for Ireland and no such problems were experienced with assembly, as they were beautifully made 98cc Zigolo 2-stroke and Galletto 4-stroke models.

In 1955 he travelled to Monza Italy at the invitation of Piero Taruffi to have a gallop on Geoff Duke's Gilera. It was his first experience of streamlining.

Then in 1956 whilst on holiday in Davos, Switzerland, he returned to Italy to give his impressions of the world's most advanced racing motorcycle – the Moto Guzzi V8. It was a revelation with its surging power and a top speed of 160 mph. He had to exercise considerable restraint whilst riding and remains the only man outside the Moto Guzzi Equipe to ride the fabulous V8. This trip had been arranged by 'Motor Cycling' with Ing Giulio Carcano, the machine's designer.

Unfortunately, Moto Guzzi's withdrawal from racing the following year brought the V8 project to a halt.

Stanley aboard James with niece Heather Burney

Patland Cup Rocky Valley 1954 on Sun

In 1957, the Golden Jubilee of the TT, after landing at Ronaldsway airport for practice week he was presented by Moto Guzzi with a new Lodola 175cc OHC model with only 100 miles. After careful running in during that two week Island holiday he found it's steering, braking, general controllability and sparkling performance of a type he had never expected to find in a lightweight machine. He was asked what he thought of it and could he sell it, but after learning the price ex works, he explained they could not be imported and sold at a competitive price.

Moto Guzzi asked "How much could you sell it for?" After he mentioned a figure, they agreed to let him have them for that price. This resulted in a substantial discount and the first order for 25

Gilera 4 at Monza

Stanley's 175 Moto Guzzi Lodola

Lodola machines arrived which were a slightly different model and colour.

Still at the 1957 TT, it had been arranged with Moto Guzzi to loan him a racing 350 – 18 years after his retirement – fitted with full frontal streamlining and equipped with pannier petrol tanks to enable the 264 miles of the Junior TT race to be covered without refuelling, the weight of the machine being only 240lbs.

About ten minutes before the ACU offices were about to close, with only a junior member of staff on duty, he signed on as a reserve rider. Next morning wearing an 'A' Plate and before the Senior Stewards realised what was happening, he had completed two laps. They called him into the office and asked *"Are you serious?"*

He explained that he was doing it for an article for 'The Motor Cycle' and that he intended to do another two laps in the afternoon.

The Stewards agreed that it would be OK, as long as it ended there.

Stanley, entered as reserve rider

1960s

Throughout the late 1950s and early 1960s he enjoyed swimming in the sea near his home and continued to travel to Switzerland for skiing.

One day while going up on the ski lift a young German man remarked *"There's a famous name"* looking at Stanley's skis . Who, he replied *"Heads?"* *"No Stanley Woods"*.

Stanley, who normally looked after the motorcycle side of the business, got a circular from Moto Guzzi advising all concessionaires that if a customer wanted to fit a windscreen to a Zigolo model, the company would provide a reinforced handlebar. Within a short period a young man whose father had bought him such a bike had decided to fit a windscreen and the handlebar broke which caused him to crash. His father was the duty sergeant at the police station within Phoenix Park and there was hell to pay.

Stanley resolved the situation by letting him have a new 235 OHV Lodola model at cost, this being what the young man had wanted in the first place.

During the early '60s the company imported a few race kits for the OHC 175 Lodola, to enable local riders

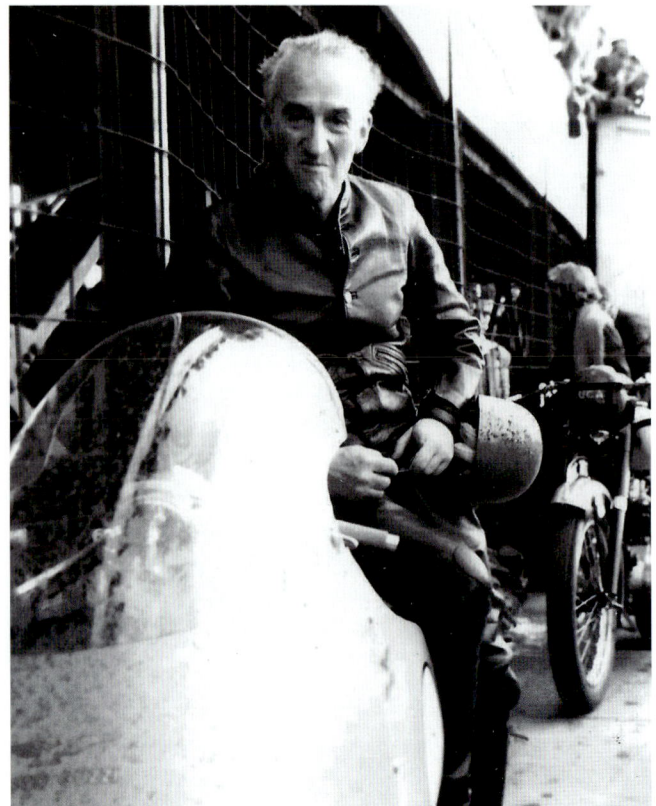

Moto Guzzi V8, Monza 1956

Ballagh Bridge, 1957

Stanley and Mildred at Davos

to compete in the 200cc Class of racing in Ireland. These were expensive (a set of close ratio gears cost £12 and a compete kit reputed to retailed for £65) and had to be ordered through Sig. Carcano.

A young Dublin rider Paul Conran won the 200 cc Class of the Skerries 100 road race on his (Kitted) Guzzi in 1961. Many years later two young men were pushing a Lodola to the line at an Irish race, when a voice from behind remarked *"You're wasting your time"*. Looking around they recognised Stanley. *"You will be at a great disadvantage without a race kit"* he continued.

"Where will get one of them" asked the boys. *''Well, I have not been able to get one for some time now but*

give me your name and address and I see what I can do."

About two months later one of them got a call from Stanley inviting them to come to his home as a carton had arrived from Italy. His first thought was 'how many months wages is this going to cost? 'When collecting the parcel he asked *"How much do we owe Mr Woods?"* Only to be told there was no charge that Moto Guzzi did not have one but had taken the parts off one of the engines in their museum; though Stanley suggested that he should pay the postage.

That tells us of the esteem that Stanley was held in by that company.

They continued to sell Moto Guzzis and could supply any make of motorcycle, but Moto Guzzi remained the preferred marque. With competition in the car market, profit on a Morris Minor and Mini was only £25. Stanley referred to it as £5 a wheel!

In 1966 they decided to sell up the business and premises which was bought by Reg Armstrong Motors who were assemblers of NSU cars and motorcycles (later Opel cars and Honda motorcycles)

He was invited to stay on for a time but with new brands in the showrooms Stanley asked Reg what he should do with the Moto Guzzi spares. Reg replied, *"Take them home and anyone seeking such spares can contact you direct"*.

In 1967 Stanley returned to the Island and was the first to congratulate Mike Hailwood on his 11th TT win, which broke his own 28 year old record.

During a motorcycle trial in Dublin Hills in 1968, now riding a Bultaco he took a couple of heavy falls in which his left hand slammed against the ground. Afterwards he noticed that the hand was flexing better for the first time since the accident in Belgium in 1938,

because the fall had broken the adhesion that had restricted movement for all those years.

He had a new hip joint fitted in Dublin hospital in 1968.

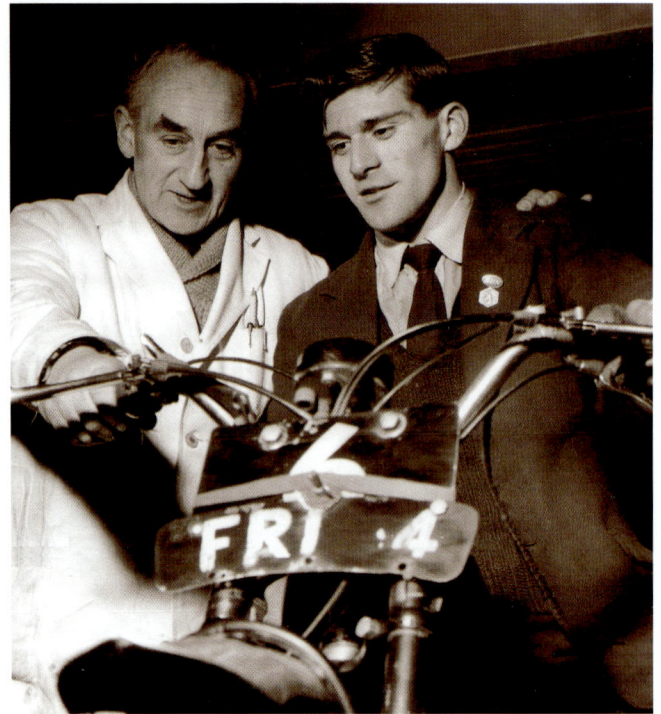

Stanley and employee Joe White with Works Sun

Andersthorp GP Circuit Stanley reunited with a 1935 Husqvarna Twin

Reg Armstrong with Stanley

CHAPTER TEN
1970-2003

1970s

AFTER RETIREMENT MILDRED was feeling a bit lonely and they decided to move to Northern Ireland in 1974, to be near her sister Nora and her family. They bought an old farmhouse next the sea at Minerstown, Co. Down with a great view of the Mountains of Mourne.

Stanley's friend Raymond Waddell made 12 return trips with his van from Dublin with Guzzi spares etc., these were imported into the North, along with his personal effects, with no duty payable providing he did not sell anything for two years.

30 MCC members Stanley, Jimmy Mooney, Arthur Owens and Jim Switzer

March 1978, Stanley's last visit to Moto Guzzi

Not long after arriving in their new home he had to have another hip replacement and when he recovered he joined the local old bike club in Belfast – The Thirty Motorcycle Club of Ulster.

By mid '70s customers were reduced to a few enthusiasts mostly in England some in the Republic of Ireland and myself, with certain spares getting scarce.

In early March 1978 he invited me to travel with him by road to Mandello Del Lario the home of Moto Guzzi, on a spares finding mission.

We were entertained by ex-factory rider Duilio Agostini the local Moto Guzzi concessionaire and his family, were given an escorted visit to the factory which had long disposed of all the old spares to other local dealers. We stayed at the Albergo Giardinetto where Stanley and other riders had been accommodated by Moto Guzzi over the years. Having had excellent weather we arrived home on St Patricks Day with his Mazda car full to the brim of spares.

Millennium year 1979 represented 1,000 years of continuous government on the Isle of Man. As part of the celebrations it was decided during TT Week to hold a 'Lap of Honour' with invitations to all well known riders of the past. Stanley was very excited when asked by Ivan Rhodes to ride his 500cc racing Velocette. The problem was that a 500 was also promised to Bill Lomas, but the situation was resolved when Ivan completed another similar machine for Bill, in record time.

John Surtees and Phil Read (MV's) led the parade, Georg Meier No 8 (Super Charged BMW). Stanley, who was No 28, asked me to attend him and he got a good start, but I was very worried while he was away. I noticed that he finished before Georg Meier and asked him afterwards *"Where did you pass Meier?" "Did I"* was his reply *"It must have been the only time that I ever passed him"* He also recalled that in pre-war days that at Glen Vine there was always a smell of wild garlic

"I smelt that smell today as I rode past" he said *"for the first time since 1939 and it brought a tear to my eye"*

1980s

The Parade proved so popular that it was decided to hold another the following year as 'Cavalcade of History'. Starting in pairs it was Stanley Woods No 1 (Velocette 500) and Mike Hailwood No 2 (FI Ducati) who led the parade. Just before the start Mike came and put his arm around Stanley's shoulder and said, *"Well Stanley I guess that you and I have earned the right to be here today".*

Stanley continued to ride the Velocette in Island parades and at events in England such

The Author, Stanley and Jim Cunningham, Lake Como, March 1978

as Mallory and Donington. Mildred was not so keen on him taken part in such events, for her health was beginning to fail. Her sister Nora would stay with her when Stanley was away, then Nora had taken ill.

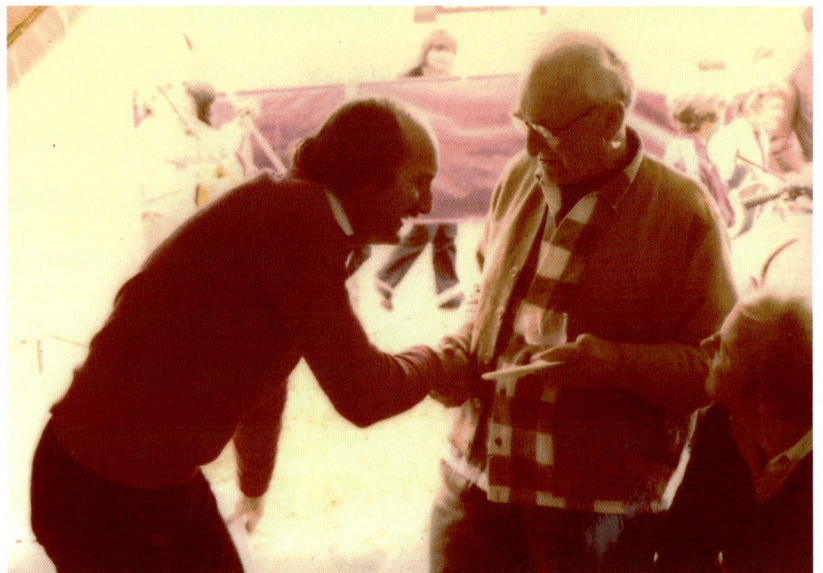

TT 1979, Mike Hailwood bows to Stanley

Stanley, Mike and David Crawford Junior

1980 TT CAVALCADE OF HISTORY

Stanley and Chris Williams at Jurby

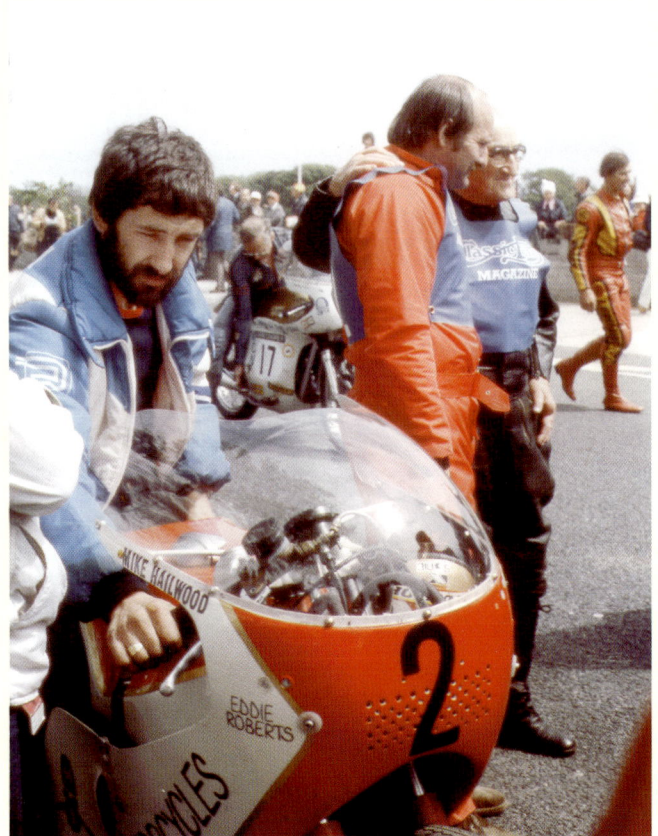

Steve Wynn warms Ducati, Mike and Stanley pose for photo

1980 TT Lap Start

Stanley has a final word with the author

Sulby Bridge

1982 TT Parade

Another early gallop on Gunnar Karlsson's Hetlund

1982 After Lap at TTRA

Bray Hill

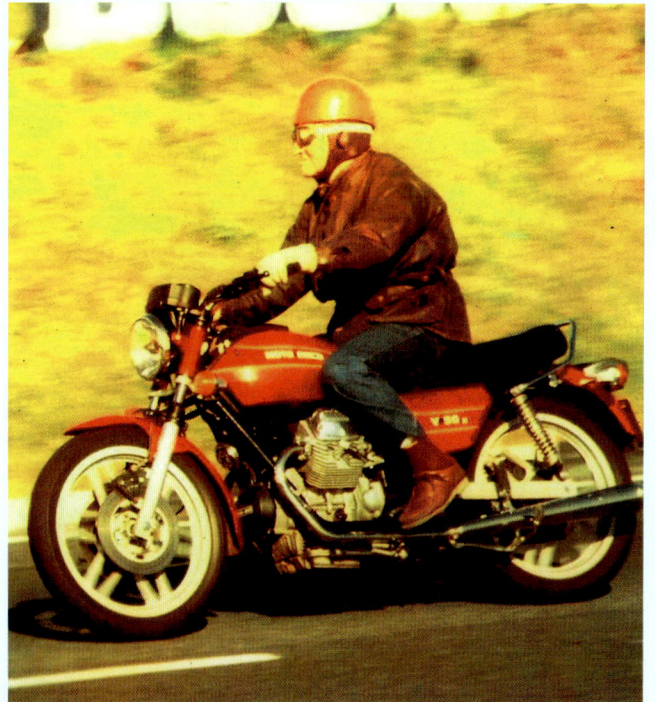

Early morning practise on V50 Moto Guzzi

1981 LAP OF HONOUR

Ivan Rhodes, Graham Crosby, Bill Lomas and Stanley at Jurby

Start of Parade

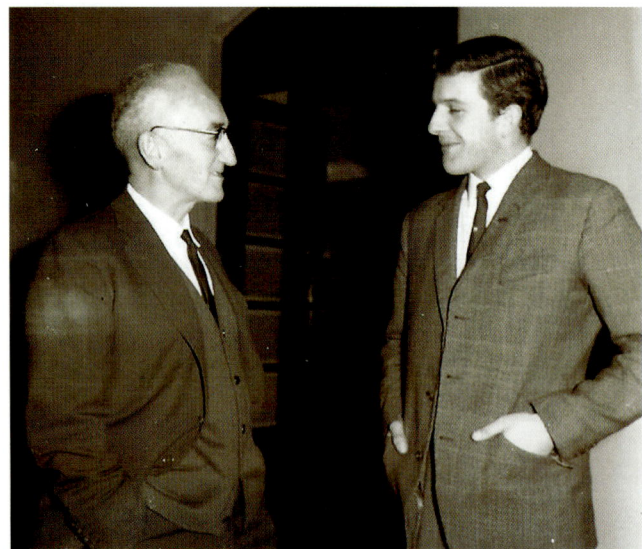

Fanta Stastny holds his No 1 plate against Stanley

Earlier picture of Stanley and Phil Read at Club Dinner

Phil Read (No 3) Stanley (No 5) Mike Hailwood Day, Donnington 11th July, 1982

In 1983 Stanley rode in the June parade and at the 50th Anniversary of the Manx GP. Actually, he was all ready to go when he was told that because he never competed in the Amateur TT or the Manx GP, he could not ride – however, with Mick Grant, he got a lap in between the races.

That was his last ever ride on a motorcycle!

One evening Mildred could not climb the stairs and a bed was brought downstairs where it remained. Stanley, 80 years old, single-handedly took care of her for the next 5 years.

One person who deserves special mention, Mr Bobby Rea of Minerstown who died in August 2011 was a local farmer who shared the lane with Stanley to gain access to his fields. They became great friends and Stanley had a wooden board with SOS painted on it. He would leave it outside as a signal for Bobby to call as he passed on his tractor. Bobby was there for them during those difficult times to run errands, do little jobs, often sitting with Mildred in the early hours after tending to his lambs. I know through conversations with Stanley that he held Bobby in the highest regard.

The Ulster Folk and Transport Museum acquired his trophy collection he was always concerned about security and was glad to see them in a new home, replacing them in the 'Trophy Room' with a pool table.

One evening in early 1986 he had a fall outside the sheds where he kept the motorcycle spares; part of the original artificial hip had broken off in the top of the femur bone.

Later when the museum officially opened 'The Stanley Woods Exhibition' he was in a wheelchair. Freddy Frith and Jock West were to attend but Freddie took ill and John Surtees came in his place. Dr Gordon Hadfield a famous orthopaedic surgeon heard of Stanley's plight and arranged for him to travel to London to have an operation.

In the spring of 1988 Ian Ledger, the Moto Guzzi singles specialist bought Stanley's spares. I met him off the Liverpool boat and set off for Minerstown. Ian's

1980, Tom Shimmin and Stanley in Trophy Room, Minerstown

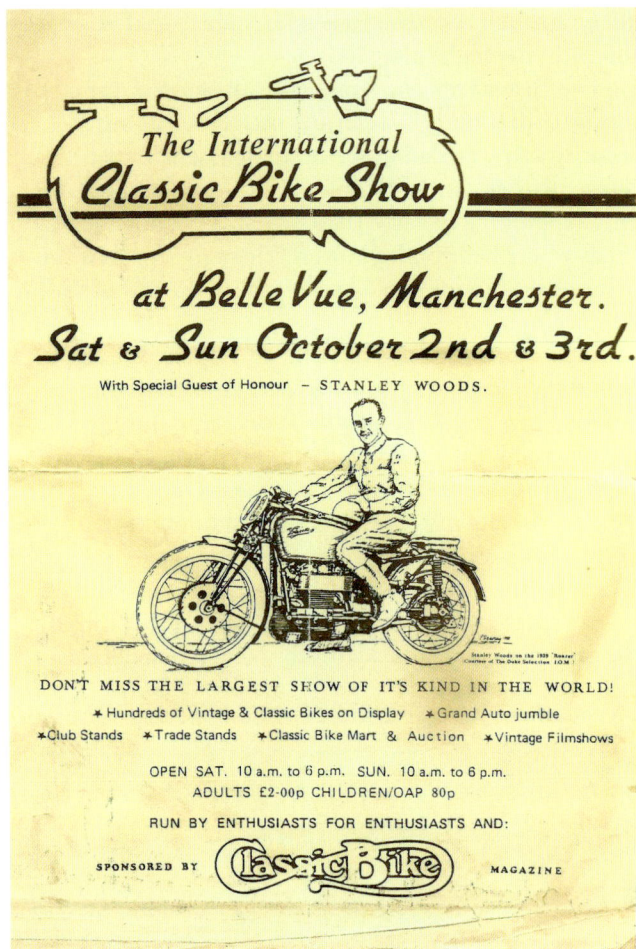

The International Classic Bike Show

at Belle Vue, Manchester.

Sat & Sun October 2nd & 3rd.

With Special Guest of Honour – STANLEY WOODS.

DON'T MISS THE LARGEST SHOW OF IT'S KIND IN THE WORLD!

✳ Hundreds of Vintage & Classic Bikes on Display   ✳ Grand Auto jumble
✳ Club Stands   ✳ Trade Stands   ✳ Classic Bike Mart & Auction   ✳ Vintage Filmshows

OPEN SAT. 10 a.m. to 6 p.m.   SUN. 10 a.m. to 6 p.m.
ADULTS £2-00p   CHILDREN/OAP 80p

RUN BY ENTHUSIASTS FOR ENTHUSIASTS AND:

SPONSORED BY Classic Bike MAGAZINE

Stanley with Charlie Manders, TTRA Lunch 1988

Norman Scott, Stanley and C. A. R. Shillington

Robert Dunlop, Stanley and Phillip McCallum, Ulster GP Offices, Belfast

Bill Lomas & Stanley with Club President, Agusto Farneti

Two of Moto Guzzi greatest riders Bill Lomas & Stanley

'Destry Rides Again'

English journalist Mike Nicks interviews Stanley at Misano

large van could only hold half the stock. Later, Stanley and I filled another van and met Ian at the NEC Birmingham while Stanley was attending the TT Riders Association lunch.

About a week later I noticed a small carton of spares addressed to a customer in South Africa. As I was one of a party going there to take part in a motorcycle event, I suggested that I should take it with me and always reckoned that was the last act of an association with Moto Guzzi which started for Stanley in 1933.

Sadly, Mildred Woods died in August 1988 and Stanley was left living alone with his beloved cats. Rex McCandless who had revolutionised motorcycle steering with his 'Featherbed frame' lived nearby and got him involved with the making of blackberry wine.

Stanley also proved very popular on the Dublin RTE 'Late Late Show', back on his feet but using crutches, he

TESTIMONIAL DINNER TO HONOUR
STANLEY WOODS

THE ROYAL HOTEL, DUN LAOGHAIRE
CO. DUBLIN
SATURDAY APRIL 1st 1989

Director and Producer Alistar Spence chats to Stanley during filming

Peter Kneale and Jack Wood from Isle of Man present Stanley with Sword of State

Testimonial Dinner

was interviewed by legendary host Gaye Byrne, himself a motorcycle enthusiast.

In June 1989 Stanley was invited by the il Velocifero Club to be their special guest at the 'Moto Storiche in Grand Prix' at Misano Italy with me as his companion. He decided he wanted to visit Venice once more, so the following day we hired a car and drove firstly to Bergamo to the motorcycle shop of Angelo Tadini, to collect some pre-war Moto Guzzi spares for me. Next morning it was off to Misano on the Adriatic Sea. On the

ON AIR MINISTRY APPROVED LIST

TELEGRAMS:
VELOCE, BIRMINGHAM.
CODES BENTLEY'S

TELEPHONE:
SPRINGFIELD 1145
(PRIVATE BRANCH EXCHANGE)

The Velocette
MOTORCYCLE

WINNER OF EIGHT
JUNIOR T.T. RACES.

MANUFACTURERS AND PATENTEES

1926	1928	1929
1938	1939	1947
1948	∿	1949

REFERENCES

OURS

YOURS

VELOCE LIMITED
P.O. BOX No. 275
HALL GREEN WORKS · YORK ROAD
HALL GREEN, BIRMINGHAM, 28
CONSIGN ALL GOODS TO HALL GREEN STATION
All communications to be addressed to the Company and not to individuals

Stanley Woods,
"Testimonial Dinner,"
Dun Laoghaire,
Eire.

April 1st 1989.

Dear Stanley,

May I on behalf of Beske & myself as ex directors of the now defunct Velocette Motor cycle Company. pass on to you our most sincere good wishes on this your Testimonial Dinner. I would also like to render our thanks for the way you advised the company on the shortcomings of the Velocette before you signed up to ride it ie 1/ Will not steer, 2/ Incorrect Gear Ratios & 3/ No Brakes. This advice, together with your ability as a rider allowed Veloce to return from the wilderness to begin winning TT races again. — Our congratulations to a superb rider & a great character. sincerely, Peter Goodman

F.20

first day of the event the club officials invited Stanley to sit on a Moto Guzzi 500 Twin, the type he had ridden in 1935 and everyone posed for some photos. He looked over at me and said *"Destry rides again."*

I never stopped laughing all day, for that was the name of a famous 1939 comedy western movie starring James Stewart and Marlene Dietrich.

At a reception held in his honour the following evening, 800 people attended including John Surtees, Bill Lomas, Carlo Ubbiali and Umberto Masetti. Stanley captivated the audience by speaking to them in perfect Italian.

We had left the hire car at Rimini Airport and the club provided us with a taxi for the several hundred miles back to Venice to catch our flight home.

It was 1st April 1989 that Joe Wood, a well known Dublin ex-road racer, chose to arrange 'A Testimonial Dinner in honour of Stanley Woods' in the Royal Hotel at Dun Laoghaire in Co Dublin, which was a sell out and attended by people from all over the world. In the presence of the Lord Mayor of Dublin he was presented with a replica Manx Sword of State by a delegation from the Isle of Man, headed by the legendary race commentator Peter Kneale.

Stanley thanked the Isle of Man government and people for their magnificent tribute and said it had been the most emotional moment of his entire life.

He returned to the Island during TT Week, for the last time, for the filming of part of the BBC film 'Stanley Woods the Movie',

Johnny Boyd was a close friend and a local surgeon, who had operated on him twice in recent years. As I left after a visit one cold Saturday evening I met Johnny at the top of the lane who was dropping by to keep an eye on Stanley. He told me later that when he had asked when he had last eaten he could not remember, so Johnny immediately got him admitted to Downpatrick hospital.

1990-2003
He recovered for a while, still attending functions, giving talks to clubs, raising funds for the TT Riders Association and for the local orthopaedic hospital he even took part in the National Great Hip Walk.

Having been the oldest person to take part and raised a large amount of money he was invited to accompany a Senior Surgeon from Musgrave Park Hospital Belfast to

Great Hip Walk

a reception in the presence of Her Majesty Queen Elizabeth the Queen Mother to mark the success of the 1991 Hip Walk at the Royal College of Surgeons in London.

Rex McCandless died in June 1992. Stanley had visited him during his residency at Corriwood Nursing home in Castlewellan Co Down and liked the place, so made it known that he should also end his days there.

Stanley died peacefully at Corriwood Nursing home on the 28th July 1993 just a few months short of his 90th birthday.

His funeral took place the following Saturday at Roselawn Crematorium Belfast. The pall bearers who held him shoulder high were Ernie Lyons, Harry Lindsay, Ivan Rhodes and I. It was not only the shortest but his slowest journey of all – he would have had something to say about that! He had always made it clear that he did not want a religious service of any kind just friends to say a few words.

On 8th June 1994 the Lieutenant Governor of the Isle of Man, His Excellency Air Marshall Sir Laurence Jones KCB, AFC, CJ. Mgt unveiled the 'Stanley Woods' clock and a plaque, facing the starting line on the TT course, which was inscribed: 'In memory of an outstanding sportsman winner of 10 TT races between 1922 and 1939 and a recipient of the Manx 'Sword of State'.

In November 2003 over 100 of his friends and acquaintances gathered in the lounge of the Minerstown Tavern opposite his old home to celebrate the 100th anniversary of his birth. There was music, talks, a display of photographs, memorabilia and motorcycles.

Today his memory is still alive throughout the world where motorcycles are spoken of and for me knowing him was a great time in my life.

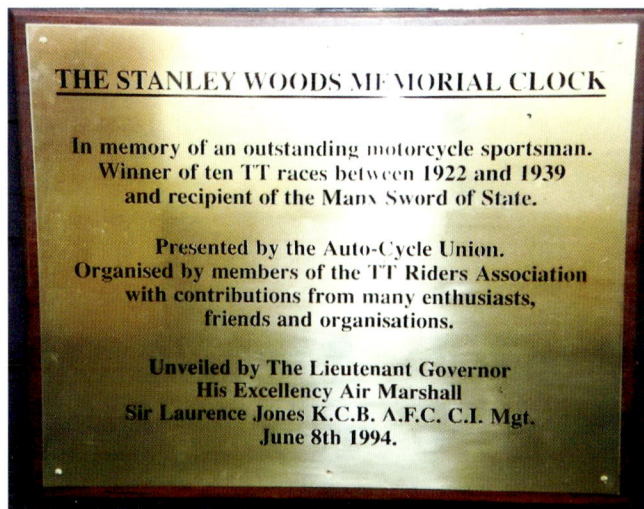

THE STANLEY WOODS MEMORIAL CLOCK

In memory of an outstanding motorcycle sportsman.
Winner of ten TT races between 1922 and 1939
and recipient of the Manx Sword of State.

Presented by the Auto-Cycle Union.
Organised by members of the TT Riders Association
with contributions from many enthusiasts,
friends and organisations.

Unveiled by The Lieutenant Governor
His Excellency Air Marshall
Sir Laurence Jones K.C.B. A.F.C. C.I. Mgt.
June 8th 1994.

Joan Crawford remembers Stanley at Roselawn

Last visit to Island

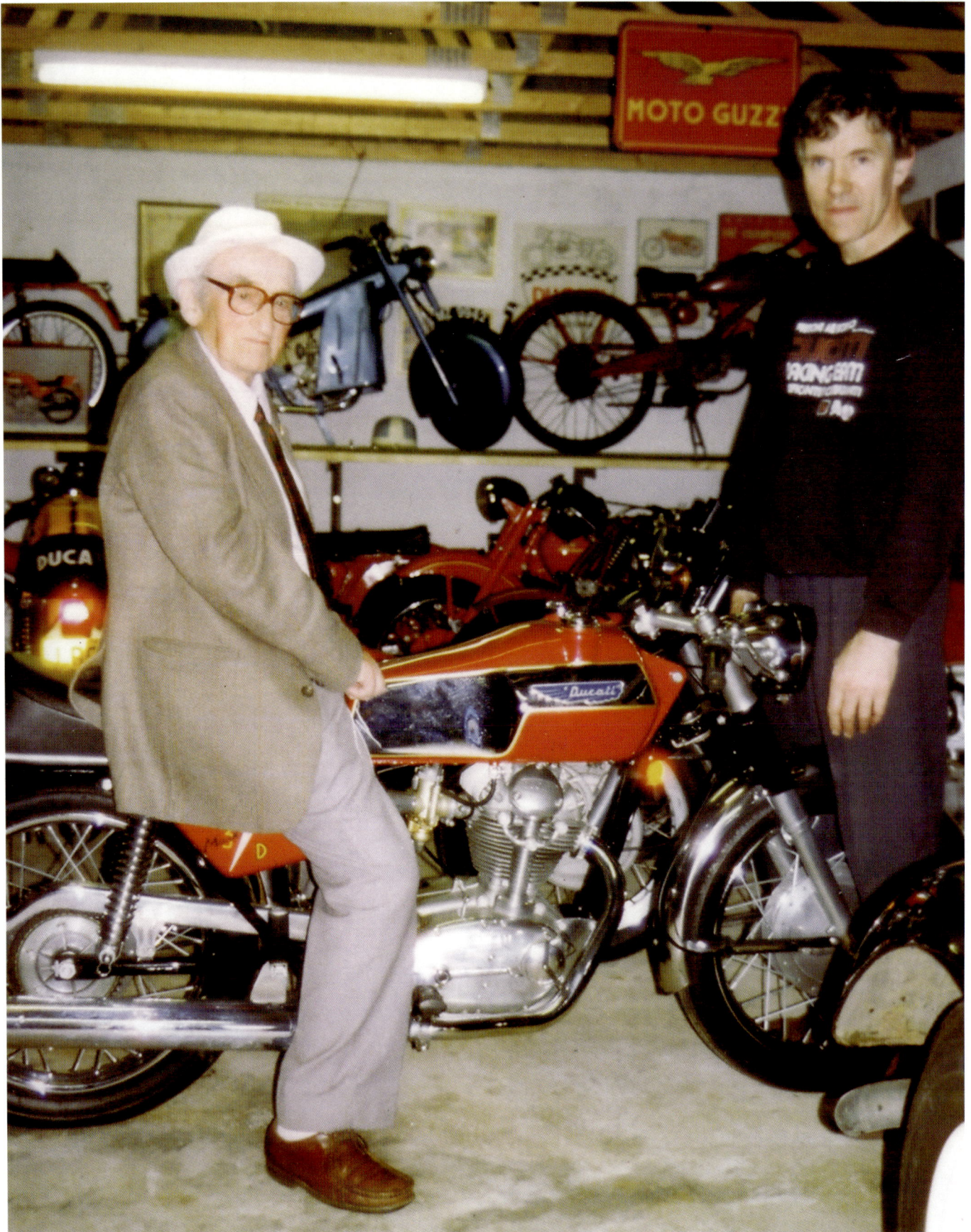

Stanley on a visit to author's home